Stay Out of My Hair!
Parenting Your Child with Trichotillomania

by
Suzanne Mouton-Odum, Ph.D.
Ruth Golomb, L.C.P.C.

Goldum Publishing

Publisher's Note

This book is designed to provide information regarding the subject matter covered. It contains only the information available to the authors at the time of the printing. Furthermore, it is sold with the understanding that the authors and publisher are not engaged in rendering psychiatric, psychological, medical or other professional services to the reader. If such services are required, they should be sought from a competent, licensed professional in the appropriate field.

To our husbands and children
with love,
Brian, Alex and Hayes
Jon, Nikki and Jacob

Table of Contents

Acknowledgements

Thank you to the Trichotillomania Learning Center and especially Christina Pearson for the endless support of the therapeutic work we do. The field of trich would still be in infancy if not for the tireless work of the TLC Board, staff, and supporters. We are thankful for the community of professionals who have been united through TLC, as well as the amazingly courageous sufferers who have been willing to share their stories, frustrations, and lives with us. Each one of you has impacted the field, the development of clinical interventions, and us personally. Thank you specifically to the families who were willing to share their stories with us for the purpose of this project. We believe that writing about real people and their unique histories lends an irreplaceable richness to the book. We know that the details you shared with us will undoubtedly enrich and heal others around the world experiencing similar frustrations. To you we are truly grateful.

A special thanks to those individuals who read, gave feedback, and helped to edit our book. Thank you to Mindy Stanley, Dave Keuler, Sherrie Vavricheck, Marty Franklin, Charley Mansueto, and Jonathan Golomb for sharing your knowledge and giving us unwavering support, enthusiasm, and encouragement with every step of this project. Finally, thank you to all of the professionals affiliated with TLC. Just as individuals with trich feel isolated and disconnected from the "mainstream," so too can we as professionals in the trenches. What a gift it is to be associated with so many wonderful and genuine people who have provided a professional home and laughter beyond belief.

Introduction

The concept of writing a book for parents of children with trichotillomania or "trich" is one that we have discussed for some time and is, unfortunately, long overdue. Some issues that parents of children with trich encounter are unique and profoundly different than those that parents of children with other conditions may face. As a result, parents often need the support and intervention of a therapist more than the child does. As treatment providers who specialize in trich, we see hundreds of families affected by this disorder. Over the years, we have developed successful intervention programs for both children and their families.

In writing this book, we intend to present up-to-date information about trichotillomania in a format that is relevant, understandable, validating, and interesting to you, the parents of children with trich. Our first goal is to help you understand how trich may impact your emotions and/or reactions to your child and, ultimately, how it may affect the functioning of your family. Further, we will help you gain a better understanding of your child's experiences and your potential role in helping your child. Finally, we will offer concrete strategies to help you interact successfully with your child around hair pulling issues that will, in turn, improve your relationship with your child, change how your child views him/herself, and ultimately result in decreased hair pulling behavior.

As therapeutic treatment providers, we believe that it is important to understand behavior in the context of a child's unique developmental process. In other words, when treating a three-year-old with trich, therapy will address developmental issues specific to three-year-olds. Accordingly, treatment of a 12-year-old with trich will look different, even though therapy is based upon similar principles and theoretical concepts.

To help our readers understand trichotillomania and relevant issues that are present at different developmental stages, we have selected four case examples that will be illustrated throughout the book. We hope that these cases will help you identify with parents who have encountered similar struggles. The cases are interwoven throughout the book to help demonstrate the use of specific strategies and interventions, as well as to illustrate the conceptualization and treatment of trichotillomania in children of different ages.

Additionally, we will help you understand your child's experiences in having trich to nurture compassion for your child. Growing up is hard enough, but growing up with trich can complicate things for everyone. Understanding the normal developmental issues your child may be facing can help you tease out what behaviors are related to trichotillomania versus what behaviors are likely the result of normal development (i.e., not everything is trich-related).

In sum, this book will provide you with an overview of what we as researchers and clinicians know about trichotillomania. It will introduce you to strategies for managing your own emotions so that your reactions to your child's pulling will be constructive and proactive. Finally, we will provide an overview of what treatment typically looks like, appropriate treatment expectations, your role in treatment, and specific ways that you, as parents, can be most helpful to your child and to the therapeutic process.

1
Tricho-what?
Understanding the Diagnosis

The history of trich

The experience of parenting a child who pulls his/her own hair and is not able to stop can be frustrating, frightening, and very confusing to say the least. Most parents have never heard of trichotillomania and have not ever considered pulling out their own hair. To many parents, the idea of pulling out one's hair may seem unusual, painful, or even strange. Quite the contrary! Looking back through history we see that hair pulling has been around for thousands of years and is more widespread than anyone ever suspected. The ancient Egyptians commonly used tweezers (as evidenced by their surfacing at archeological digs in Egypt), suggesting that they at least pulled hair for grooming purposes. Further, there are references to hair pulling in both the Bible (Book of Ezra) and Homer's "The Illiad." Hippocrates, when describing how to interview a patient, wrote about routinely asking patients whether or not they pulled out their hair.

It was not until the late 1800's that the name trichotillomania was given to the phenomenon. A French doctor named Hallipeau was the first to clinically describe hair pulling and to give it a name. Trichotillomania is actually derived from the Greek roots: "trich" meaning "hair," "tillo" meaning "pull" or "pulling," and "mania" meaning "out of control" or "frenzy." Literally, trichotillomania means "out of control hair pulling" or a "hair pulling frenzy."

Hair pulling is commonly perceived as an outcome of feeling overwhelmed or stressed out. When a person is feeling overwhelmed or stressed with life, he or she often will say, "I could just pull my hair out!" What many people do not realize is that some individuals actually DO pull out their hair.

What is "trich?"

The Diagnostic and Statistical Manual (4th Edition) of the American Psychiatric Association (DSM-IV) defines trichotillomania as having the five following criteria:

1 Repetitive pulling of one's own hair that results in noticeable hair loss.

2 A feeling of tension prior to pulling or when trying to resist the behavior.

3 Pleasure, gratification, or relief while engaging in the behavior.

4 The behavior is not accounted for by another medical (dermatological) or psychiatric problem (such as schizophrenia).

5 The hair pulling leads to significant distress in one or more areas of the person's life (social, occupational, or work) (APA, 1994).

Although these criteria have been beneficial in describing a behavior that had previously not even been included in the DSM, they are not adequate. After studying trich and working with hundreds of people who pull out their hair, we know that many people suffering with this problem do not meet all of these criteria. For example, some people pull from parts of their body that are not visible to others (pubic area, chest, arms, legs, etc.), and the hair loss cannot be readily seen. Even though the hair loss is not "noticeable," it may still be a serious problem for them.

In addition, people report a variety of emotions other than tension prior to pulling, such as boredom, excitement, anger, frustration, guilt, and suspense. Others report that they really do not feel anything prior to pulling. In fact, many people are not even aware that they are having an urge to pull. Further, hair pulling is frequently coupled with feelings of frustration, anger, and guilt, rather than pleasure or relief. Despite the diagnostic criteria being a bit limited, what we do know is that trichotillomania is a complex and heterogeneous problem that affects different people in different ways.

Who has trich and how did my child get it?

So how widespread is this seemingly rare and unheard-of disorder? Only a handful of studies have tried to estimate the prevalence of trich, so our understanding of the total number of people who pull their hair is limited at best. Dr. Gary Christenson and his colleagues at the University of Minnesota found that 1.5% of males and 3.4% of females in a college population met the criteria for trich as defined by the DSM. However, much higher estimates have been reported for repetitive hair pulling that does not meet the full criteria for trich (without noticeable hair loss or with no reported tension-reduction cycle). For example, studies done by Dr. Melinda Stanley and Dr. Barbara Rothbaum demonstrate that despite traditional beliefs that hair pulling is both unusual and uncommon, repetitive hair pulling may affect as much as 10% to 22% of the population (tens of millions of people in the U.S. alone!). These figures may make it easier to understand that your child is certainly not alone.

Most of the research regarding trichotillomania in the past 30 years has been with adults. However, recent studies conducted by Dr. Martin Franklin in Philadelphia have focused exclusively on children with trich. Interestingly, his results do not mirror what we see in adults. For example, the female to male ratio of trich in adults is 9:1, while in children, he found the female to male ratio to be 1:1. This means that for kids, hair pulling occurs in about the same number of boys as girls.

How do we account for this huge discrepancy? Is it that adult males with trich do not talk about it? Perhaps men pull from places that are not readily noticeable to the outside world, so the pulling does not cause them problems. Maybe men experience hair pulling as a problem, but they do not seek treatment. Perhaps more boys stop pulling during adolescence and therefore do not pull in adulthood. Because the average age of onset for trich is 12-13 years of age (around puberty), it also is possible that the majority of people who begin pulling during puberty are female. As a result, the ratio switches sometime in adolescence to be predominantly female. Likely, it is some combination of all of these hypotheses.

The age at which children begin pulling ranges. Some children pull as early as six months of age, although more commonly, repetitive hair pulling begins in early adolescence. In reality, however, children can begin pulling at any age. There is no formula that describes the prognosis of trich (who will keep pulling into adulthood and who will stop) based upon the age of onset.

Many health professionals tell parents that if a young child (less than five years of age) begins to pull, he or she is likely to grow out of it. This is sometimes true, but not necessarily the case. Upon hearing this, parents may decide to ignore the behavior and perhaps not seek treatment that could benefit their child. This is unfortunate for these children because education and early intervention can be helpful for behavior change. Ignoring trich can have other implications as well. For some children, parents' ignoring of their behavior sends the message that hair pulling is a very shameful thing—something that is unspeakable.

Some children, however, do seem to grow out of it—they pull for a time, and eventually stop on their own. This does not necessarily mean, however, that their pulling will not reemerge in adolescence or at some later time in life. Consequently, parents need to know that even if childhood symptoms go away, there is still a possibility of future relapse.

Regardless of what age your child started pulling his/her hair, we believe it is important for you to educate yourself about trich and to follow the guidelines outlined in this book. In this way you will better understand your child in the context of his/her development, manage your own emotions and reactions to your child's behavior, and identify specific ways to successfully parent your child with trichotillomania.

Shhhh...it is a secret!

Despite the seemingly widespread nature of trich, most people have never heard of it or believe that it is a very rare phenomenon. Why is this? Why have most people heard of Tourette Syndrome or obsessive compulsive disorder, both of which occur far less commonly than trich, but have never heard of hair pulling? The answer is complicated. First, most people with trich do not want to tell anyone about their behavior because it is not widely talked about. Consequently, people with trich often believe that they are alone—surely no one else pulls out their own hair? Unfortunately, raising awareness would require people with trich (or parents of children with trich) to talk about having the disorder—something that may be difficult to do.

Second, there is a great deal of shame surrounding hair pulling. Sufferers are not likely to talk about hair pulling because they are ashamed of it, perhaps largely because of the self-inflicted nature of the behavior—people have bald spots that they themselves have created. It is easier to talk about diabetes or asthma because these diseases/conditions are perceived to be "out of a person's direct control." In the case of trich, however, there is the underlying perception that the person is causing the problem.

Further, misunderstandings about why people pull hair are common. In many cultures hair represents beauty, youth, health, and strength. The systematic, non-cosmetic removal of one's own hair can mistakenly imply a desire to be ugly, or of some underlying self-loathing or self-destructive tendency.

These assumptions can further promote feelings of shame and humiliation. As a result of these faulty beliefs, people with trich are often blamed for their behavior. Because it is perceived to be under their control, people with trich are often told to "just quit doing it!" This kind of response is both blaming and unhelpful to the person suffering with trich. Your child needs understanding and nurturing from you, not blame, ridicule, or punishment. As you will learn in later chapters, children pull their hair because it feels good to them or helps them meet some intrinsic need, not because they want to be ugly or because they dislike themselves.

Emotional problems in addition to trich

Often parents are concerned that if their child has trich, he/she also must have some serious underlying psychological difficulty or will eventually develop other, more serious, psychological problems. Recent research on childhood trichotillomania conducted by Dr. Franklin and his colleagues shows that children with trich are no more likely to have another psychological disorder than children who don't have trich. However, findings from studies conducted with adults show that those with trich are more likely to suffer from depression and certain anxiety disorders, such as generalized anxiety disorder (excessive worry).

In other words, children with trich tend to be free of other psychological problems, while adults seem to suffer from more depression and anxiety. Why is this? We can hypothesize that if one has struggled unsuccessfully for many years with trich, one may become depressed and/or feel overly anxious about certain areas of one's life. This is probably the most important reason why we encourage parents to educate themselves and to intervene early in their child's life—to prevent suffering and hardship later. Supporting and nurturing your child will encourage the development of a positive self-image and greater self-worth.

Studies have demonstrated that there is a higher rate of certain psychological disorders among family members of individuals with trich. Family members of people with trich are more likely to have a diagnosis of trich, obsessive compulsive disorder, Tourette Syndrome, anxiety disorders, depression, and other body focused repetitive behaviors, such as skin picking, nail biting, thumb sucking, cheek or lip biting, cuticle picking, or tooth grinding. Oftentimes at the initial intake session, parents will say something like "No one in our family has ever done anything like this," while at the same time they are biting their nails. Parents who are self-aware and take time to examine their own habits and behaviors are better able to develop empathy for their child and his/her experiences.

Sometimes when talking to parents, we use examples of habits that are hard to change that they might better relate to, like overeating or smoking. For example, have you ever ordered a hamburger instead of a salad, knowing that the salad would be healthier? Have you ever tried to quit smoking or to give up caffeine?

With this in mind, take a minute to consider any behaviors that you or your family members engage in that are both unhealthy and difficult to change. Does anyone in your family or your spouse's family bite their fingernails, bite their lip or the inside of their cheek, pick their cuticles, fingernails, or skin (acne, mosquito bites, scabs, calluses), overeat, smoke, or crack their knuckles? More than likely they do. Have you ever tried to change any of these behaviors yourself? If so, was it difficult? Were you successful? Was it ever frustrating for you to make these changes? Did you ever experience failure? Are you starting to understand?

Although these behaviors can be more socially acceptable and may not result in the physical changes that hair pulling can, they are similar to trich in that they are hard behaviors to change. If you have ever tried, you know first-hand that it is not easy to break a habit and that it requires motivation, readiness, energy, hard work, and support from those around you.

Is this self-mutilation?

Trichotillomania is a disorder that is tremendously misunderstood by the public, as well as by those who suffer. Recently there have been postings on the Internet stating that hair pulling is in the same category as, or ultimately leads to, self-injurious cutting commonly referred to as "self-mutilation." There are no scientific data to support this assertion and, in fact, trich and self-mutilation seem to involve quite different processes. People who pull out their hair do it because it feels good, not because they want to harm or disfigure themselves. People who cut or otherwise injure themselves often describe wanting to feel physical pain as opposed to emotional pain. The self-injury may help them to "drown out" the emotional pain. In other words, the processes underlying each may be completely different; thus, we would argue that they are categorically different behaviors.

Of course my child wants to stop pulling...I think

Frequently, individuals come to treatment stating, "I really want to stop pulling my hair." Upon further investigation by a trained therapist, these same individuals will admit that they do not really want to stop pulling, but desire to grow back their hair, so they feel like they should stop. In other words, people like to pull hair, but they do not like the outcome of pulling (bald patches or thinning of the hair). Simply put, for many people hair pulling feels good! A parallel example might be "I like eating chocolate cake, but I do not like the way it makes me feel or look. Sometimes, though, I still choose to eat it, even though I know it will cause me to gain weight." This ambivalence is, perhaps, something that most of us can relate to and helps us understand the complex feelings that a child may experience when pulling hair.

When working with children, it is especially important to gauge the children's level of ambivalence or confusion about changing their behavior. It is possible that you are more motivated than your child is to stop pulling. These feelings can be quite confusing to your child and also very frustrating for you. How these complicated situations are handled by the therapist and the parents can have a significant impact on the parent-child relationship and on the ultimate success of the therapy. Chapters 4 and 5 will provide specific tools for you to better understand your child's feelings about trich, as well as strategies for helping him/her to feel less confused and more empowered to change.

Trich as a part of a larger class of disorders: body focused repetitive behaviors

It may be that trich is part of a larger umbrella of related disorders we refer to as body focused repetitive behaviors (BFRBs). As mentioned earlier, examples of other BFRBs include nail biting, thumb sucking, skin picking, lip biting, cheek biting, cuticle picking, nail picking, tooth grinding, and knuckle cracking. These behaviors are often thought of as simple "nervous habits." However, if you have ever tried to stop doing a BFRB, you already know that the behavior is neither simple nor easily discarded. As stated earlier in this chapter, it is common for people who have trich to also have one or more of these other BFRBs. What we know about BFRBs is that they are more than just "bad habits"; they are complex behaviors that are started and reinforced by many internal and external forces. We will discuss all of these "forces" in Chapter 7, as well as how therapy can specifically address them.

Is trich the result of trauma?

Some therapists mistakenly assume that children begin to pull out their hair as the result of a traumatic or negative event. This way of thinking is inspired by the school of psychoanalysis which teaches that behaviors and anxieties are manifestations of deeper, unresolved issues from childhood that are creeping up from the subconscious into the conscious life. However, only 50% of people with trich report a negative event occurring at the time their hair pulling began. Further, negative events can be such things as "moving to a new town," "changing schools," "parents divorcing," or "losing a friend." The other 50% report no stressor at the time of pulling onset. Thus, it is erroneous to assume that trich is the result of some negative or stressful event that your child has experienced, but perhaps not verbalized.

How genes play a part

Research has not yet demonstrated why hair pulling manifests in one person and not in another. There seems to be a family correlation with trich, meaning that if one person in the family has trich there is a higher likelihood that another person will also have it. However, we see cases all the time where a child has trichotillomania and there seems to be no other person in the family who suffers from it. When we look at the incidence of other BFRBs in the families of people with trich, we see a higher correlation. As stated earlier, hair pulling may be part of this larger category of behaviors. Not only do we see a higher incidence of BFRBs in family members of people with trich, we also see a higher incidence of them in people who have trich. Up to 40% of people who pull hair also engage in some type of skin picking behavior. As a result, treatment of trichotillomania oftentimes includes the treatment of other BFRBs as well.

Common theories about trich

To understand trichotillomania and the various theories that have been used to describe the behavior, it is useful to take an historical perspective. As mentioned earlier, one of the first theories describing trichotillomania was the psychoanalytic theory. In keeping with this perspective, trich was initially described as the result of a trauma or an unresolved psychosexual issue that manifested in pulling behavior. Treatment, therefore, was aimed at resolving the "issue," thus eliminating the need to pull. What therapists trained in this theory ultimately learned was that often, despite resolution of issues, hair pulling remained constant. Also, many people presented for treatment with relatively few issues and described a normal, loving, uneventful childhood experience. As a result, new theories began to arise to describe the onset and course of hair pulling behavior.

Trichotillomania also has been understood to be a disorder of habit. This theory, developed by Nathan Azrin and R. Gregory Nunn, serves as the basis for a treatment called Habit Reversal Therapy (HRT). This habit theory posits that hair pulling begins spontaneously or is learned, then becomes associated with a variety of cues and contexts which perpetuate the behavior. For example, if a person pulls his/her hair every time he or she talks on the phone, pulling or thinking of pulling will become a habit when the phone is raised to the ear. Strategies are taught to "compete" with hair pulling behavior in these situations. Although this theory does a good job of explaining and addressing certain aspects of hair pulling behavior, it does not adequately describe the entire spectrum of hair pulling triggers and cues.

Theorists also have looked to the animal world to understand trichotillomania. Similar pulling or plucking behavior is seen in cats, dogs, monkeys, birds, and mice. What is unclear, however, is whether or not a bird that plucks her feathers or a monkey who pulls his fur actually has trichotillomania. Recently, scientists have identified the part of the genetic code in mice that, when mutated, will cause the offspring of that mouse to chew its fur off. This breakthrough caused many people to become interested in the possibility of finding a genetic cause for trich, which may ultimately lead to a cure. However, although hair pulling behavior appears to be similar in animals, researchers cannot be sure that the behavior observed in these animals is indeed trichotillomania.

Cognitive behavioral theorists have applied their theory to trich and have been more comprehensive in explaining and understanding hair pulling behavior. In fact, this book focuses on the principles of Cognitive Behavioral Therapy (CBT) that explain and guide the treatment of trichotillomania. CBT integrates a person's beliefs or thoughts (cognitions) with behavioral experiences, such as positive or negative reinforcers to explain why a behavior begins and persists.

Dr. Charles Mansueto and his colleagues at the Behavior Therapy Center of Greater Washington have utilized the principles of CBT to expand the earlier work in Habit Reversal Therapy as it applies to trichotillomania. Dr. Mansueto's approach is referred to as the Comprehensive Behavioral Approach or "ComB" approach. The ComB model is used to evaluate a person's unique cognitive and behavioral experiences that serve to reinforce hair pulling and to build a behavioral analysis or functional analysis to explain what purpose the hair pulling serves for that individual. As stated earlier, people pull hair because it feels good or otherwise helps them meet certain needs. This comprehensive analysis explains how hair pulling meets these needs, which then opens the door to finding individualized coping strategies to help that person to stop pulling.

Many components contribute to the development of behavioral patterns that may result in hair pulling behavior. These components include the following:

1 Sensory experiences during the pulling process

2 Thoughts or beliefs about hair, hair pulling, and what the person thinks will happen if hair is not pulled

3 Emotional experiences before, during, and after hair pulling

4 Motor behaviors or "fiddling" with one's hair either before or after the hair is pulled, often without awareness

5 Environmental cues and triggers (common places/ activities where hair pulling happens)

In gathering all of this information, a trained therapist can create a more comprehensive understanding of why a person pulls his or her hair and, more importantly, can choose strategies to help manage the behavior. All of these concepts will be discussed at length in Chapter 7.

Now that we have given you a bit of history, answered some common questions, and reviewed several theories about trichotillomania, we are going to move on. In the next chapter, we will illustrate how hair pulling can uniquely affect children and their families at different stages of development.

2
What is Happening to My Child?

Now that we have reviewed the history and literature about trichotillomania, let's look at some case examples of families dealing with a child who has trich. Some of these situations may sound familiar to you, while others may be very different than yours.

In the beginning...

Ashley

I always thought it was cute the way little Ashley sucked her thumb and twirled her hair. She had been doing that for as long as I could remember. But when she was about two, I noticed a bald spot where she twirled her hair. Soon the bald spot spread and I noticed that she was pulling out her hair and twisting it around her thumb while she sucked. Was I doing something wrong? Was I causing her to pull out her hair? At first I freaked out. I started to tell her "No!" when she even touched her head. I lectured, I bribed, I cried, I punished, and I yelled.

Charles and Jane are the parents of little Ashley. Like many parents, they experienced a wide range of emotions when they first realized that Ashley was pulling out her hair. Being a parent is the most rewarding, perplexing, wonderful, confusing, and humbling job any of us will ever have. As a result, we put a lot of pressure on ourselves to be really good (dare we say "perfect") parents. Unfortunately, there is no such thing. In addition, this is one job without a job description, and every really good parent does it differently. So what is a parent to do when a child has a problem?

Oddly enough, one of the first things to do is to take care of yourself. If you are really upset, you will not be able to sift through information, speak with doctors, and make important decisions. In addition, children (even very young ones) pick up on parents' emotions and reactions. Try to stay calm and not over react.

So what do you need first? Very often the answer is to obtain good information. Start doing some research, talk to your child's pediatrician, make sure that your child's hair loss is actually due to pulling and not some other condition, find information on the Internet, and talk to mental health professionals. Find out what is going on and begin to formulate a plan. When you are the parent of a toddler or pre-school age child, much of the work is going to be guided by you (two-year-olds aren't very introspective!) It will be important for you to hear information that is given to you and to be willing to try out things at home. Finally, it is always helpful to feel supported, have good guidance, and be able to allow for the likelihood that you have done nothing to cause this behavior.

Intervention for toddlers and pre-school age children looks rather different than for those who are older. First, it's all up to you to learn how to help, support, reinforce, and modify behavior. Just like you support and guide your child at this stage deciding such behaviors as when to start potty training, give up the pacifier, or transition out of a crib into a bed, you will need to use the same parenting skills with the hair pulling. You will be the guiding force for your child at this stage of development. Fortunately, children at this age are developing and changing so rapidly that understanding how NOT to pull hair is just one other thing that the child is learning while growing up. Therefore, you need to be committed to the process, have a plan, and have energy to deal with the inevitable ups and downs as you help your child develop strategies to stop hair pulling.

Also, know that if this is not a good time for you to devote yourself to helping your child change hair pulling behavior, don't. You can always choose to work on it when you have adequate time and energy. You may want to try to ignore the behavior for a few months and see if it improves on its own. (Be aware that ignoring behavior is much harder than it sounds! However, it's a reasonable thing to try.)

Why my child?

Sarah

Sarah came home from her second grade class one day missing all of her eyelashes on one eye. I was shocked! I asked her in a panic, "What happened?" Sarah did not respond at all. When she finally did, she seemed completely confused about my question. All she said is, 'What are you talking about?' Over the next few days, all of her eyelashes disappeared. I became increasingly more worried. Sarah promised me that she had no idea what I was talking about. She noticed that eyelashes were gone, but said she had absolutely no idea what had happened. How could this be? Is she sick? Is she completely out of touch with reality? What kind of a doctor should I bring her to? Help!

Stu and Karen, Sarah's parents, quickly became worried and confused. Since Sarah seemed totally unaware of what happened to her eyelashes, her parents wondered what was wrong with her. They did not know where to turn. "Why is this happening?" and "What is happening?" were the two thoughts that kept turning round and round in Karen's head.

Sarah has trichotillomania. She is unable to tell her parents that she is actually pulling out her own eyelashes because she is so embarrassed and upset. In addition, Sarah is a very responsible, high achieving child. She feels as if she is doing something wrong and at the same time, she can't stop herself. Most of all she feels shame—shame that she is creating this problem that makes her look different. It is the worst feeling in the world for her. She continues to tell her parents that she has no idea what happened to her eyelashes because telling them the truth would be ten times worse. They are already upset enough.

Stu and Karen start to feel very strongly that Sarah is purposely lying to them. How can she truly not know what she is doing? They have walked into the room and seen her pulling at her eyelashes! Stu and Karen wonder what is happening to their precious daughter that would turn her into what they perceive as a lying, deceitful person.

This is a very challenging situation for any parent. Adding to the distress is the idea that your child may be "hurting" herself AND lying! Understanding your child's point of view may be very helpful. Children who pull their hair are, in actuality, really good kids who have found a unique and powerful way to soothe themselves. Often kids truly don't know why they pull; however, they do know that it feels good. It's hard to say whether or not these children "want" to pull. On one hand they do, because it feels good. On the other hand they don't, because they don't like to upset the family or they don't like the results of pulling—hair loss and feeling badly about themselves. Trich is a complicated problem at this stage. Therefore, to maintain the feeling of being a good person, and to avoid further upset, children often say that they are "not pulling" or "don't know how the hair came out."

It is important to provide a calm, safe environment for children to feel comfortable exploring the possibility that they might be pulling out their hair. It helps to take a "matter of fact" approach. Providing understandable information about this interesting behavior called trichotillomania is a good way to start. Talk openly with your child, and try not judge or blame him/her. In addition, provide information a little at a time to give your child time to digest the information more effectively and completely. The first time that you sit down to talk, you may be the only one talking. Additionally, at this sitting you may give only one or two small pieces of information, such as "lots of kids pull out their hair" and "children pull their hair because it feels good to them."

Most importantly, if you only do one thing during this first conversation, express to your child that you love him/her no matter what. Make it clear that hair pulling is not a deciding factor of your child's "goodness" as a human being. Your child will be tremendously relieved, and it will take some of the pressure off knowing that despite the pulling, you are still going to love and support him/her. Many parents think that "accepting" trich in their child is somehow "condoning" the behavior and therefore prolonging it. We have not found this to be true at all. Parents who take a loving approach to their children and their children's trich find that they, and their children, navigate the recovery process much more easily than those who take a more punitive approach.

Common mistaken beliefs

Hannah

Middle school is a tough time for parents in the best of circumstances, but for Peggy and Bob it became a nightmare. Hannah started to pull hair out of her scalp and pubic area when she was 12 years old. Peggy noticed that Hannah was spending more time in the bathroom in the morning. She thought that Hannah was just being a teenager and fussing with her hair. One day Hannah came downstairs crying and said, "I can't cover this spot anymore!" "What spot?" Peggy said. This was the beginning of a long hard journey. Peggy wondered what was going on in school that was causing Hannah to pull out her hair. And worse, why would she pull out her pubic hair? Does she not want to become a woman? Is she ashamed of growing up?

Peggy knew that being 12 years old was a tough time, but really! What is so bad that is causing Hannah to pull out her hair? Hannah also stopped confiding in Peggy a few years ago as she began to approach adolescence, so although Peggy knew her friends and teachers, she did not really know what was going on in Hannah's head from day to day. Was being a good student too much pressure? Were they, as her parents, expecting too much from her?

Peggy and Bob made an appointment with the school counselor and her teachers. To their amazement the teachers and the counselor had no idea that Hannah was struggling, unhappy, or pulling out her hair. They had never heard of such a thing and suggested rather judgmentally that something must be wrong at home. The counselor spoke privately with the parents after the meeting and warned Peggy and Bob that the behavior was a form of self-mutilation and that the next step for Hannah would likely be to start cutting herself.

After the meeting Peggy and Bob were absolutely beside themselves. What were they doing that was causing their child to hurt herself? Had she been abused by someone? Hannah seemed like a pretty happy, well adjusted teen. Could they be that out of touch? Peggy called the pediatrician and made an emergency appointment. After speaking with Hannah, the pediatrician concluded that this was "just a phase" and that she would simply grow out of it. If she did not grow out of it in the next few months, Peggy and Bob were told not to tolerate this behavior and to punish her every time that she pulled her hair.

Now Peggy and Bob were very confused. What should they do? Should they treat this as self-mutilation and possibly hospitalize her? Should they ignore it and hope that it goes away? Should they punish her for pulling? Many parents receive very conflicting recommendations. Finding a reliable source of information can be extremely challenging. All Peggy and Bob want is what is best for Hannah, but what is best for her?

How can parents find a reliable source of information?

Isn't the school a good source? Surely the pediatrician would know about trichotillomania! Unfortunately, many pediatricians have only a cursory understanding of trichotillomania and, depending on the age of your pediatrician, the information may be quite outdated. Well-meaning professionals sometimes are not completely current on all of the reliable information available to them.

When dealing with trich, it is important to consult with an expert, or at least someone who has experience treating people with this problem. In today's health care system, a doctor with general knowledge is usually the first stop, not the last. If you have allergies, you consult an allergist; heart problems, a cardiologist; asthma, a pulmonologist; and so on. When your child is pulling out hair, who should you consult?

A good place to start is with The Trichotillomania Learning Center (TLC), a national nonprofit organization located in Santa Cruz, California. The TLC has much useful information including brochures and resources for schools, cosmetologists, and doctors, as well as lists of therapists throughout the country who are trained to work with adults and children with trich. When you first contact a professional (the school counselor, pediatrician, etc.), ask how many children he/she has seen with this problem. Understanding a professional's experience, orientation, and training in this area will be very helpful for you to be able to assess the information given to you.

You may already have consulted with a professional and received some mistaken information. If this is the case, you are not alone. No matter what people have told you, here are some important things to remember:

1 Hair pulling is not always a symptom of an underlying problem or emotional disorder; most children who pull their hair are quite happy, well adjusted individuals.

2 Although some kids do stop pulling on their own, this is not assured. If possible, early intervention can be very helpful and is advisable.

3 Children pull because it helps them feel better in some way, or meets a need. The behavior is NOT self-abuse or an indication of underlying serious psychological disturbance.

4 In general, children do not pull because they were sexually abused, experienced a trauma, or were somehow seriously harmed.

5 Hair pulling does not predict the future onset of anything (including self-mutilation, depression, anxiety, or obsessive compulsive disorder).

6   Hair pulling is not a sign of self-hatred or a desire to be ugly. (Although, left untreated, these feelings can occur as a result of years of performing a perplexing behavior and feeling isolated, out of control, and bizarre.)

7   Hair pulling is not an easy behavior to stop without assistance. Simply telling your child to "Stop it" or "You would stop doing it if you really wanted to" feels blaming and unsupportive to him/her.

8   Punishing your child for pulling hair is never a good solution as it fosters low self-esteem and instills shame.

◉
Hayden

Hayden is in the 10th grade and has always been a shy, introspective child. He is artistic, creative, and very smart. Hayden is the "hero child" of the family, always trying to do his personal best to impress his parents and get positive feedback from them. He is the first born of three children and has always protected and watched over his younger siblings. His parents, Ellen and Fred, are loving and supportive of Hayden, but recently decided to separate due to longstanding, marital conflict. Although they did their best to keep their three children out of marital issues and discussions, sometimes Hayden was able to hear arguments late at night when they were less vigilant of their voice tone.

At 16, Hayden began to pull out his scalp hair. Because he had always been so quiet and did not share many feelings with his parents, the pulling went unnoticed for some time. Further, because he has always focused on "doing good," he was especially reticent to tell his parents what was going on. Thus, when Ellen first looked closely at the hair loss, it was quite substantial, covering most of his crown and sides of his scalp with only a thin layer of hair veiling the bald spot. Ellen remembered that when Hayden was going into kindergarten, he had experienced some bald patches, but the hair grew back by winter break and he never had another problem. She had chalked this up to alopecia and never sought treatment, but this seemed different, more severe.

At first, Ellen and Fred began to blame themselves, feeling responsible for the behavior as they were causing the "divorce," thus causing the stress. Later, they began to blame each other, using Hayden's pulling as a weapon to find fault with each other's parenting abilities. For example, when Hayden returned from visits with his father, if Ellen noticed any hair loss, she immediately attributed it to "stress at Dad's house," lending support to her argument that her former husband was "unfit."

It's important to understand that children whose parents go through a divorce have complicated feelings. Most children who experience divorce in the family, however, do not pull out their hair. At the same time, many children from happy, intact families do pull out their hair. Therefore, assuming divorce is a cause for hair pulling is unfounded.

Children start pulling out their hair for reasons that don't include stress, abuse, or trauma. Normal life events can "trigger" hair pulling. Some onset events include, but are not limited to the following:

1　Examining a hair pulled from one's head under a microscope in science class

2　Giving an eyelash as a "ticket" to join a group of friends at play

3　Making a wish on an eyelash

4　Pulling a stray or errant hair out during grooming which can awaken the desire to pull more

5　Seeing another child pull (maybe one who is popular or highly respected)

Any of these common and innocent events can set the stage for hair pulling. Although stress can exacerbate any behavior, it is not always the cause. It is important to remember that your child's pulling is not your fault, and in the case of Hayden, it is not either parent's fault. As parents, we tend to blame ourselves when things don't go the way we think they should. Hair pulling can become a way of coping with unpleasant emotions for some children, but it is not always the case. For Hayden, pulling may have happened in response to feelings of stress about his parents' divorce, or it may simply be a habit that developed over time, or some combination of the two. We cannot assume that it is either. A careful evaluation by a trained therapist will be necessary to determine how this behavior is meeting his needs. Next, a treatment plan to address these needs will need to be developed.

As you have seen, each child has a unique experience with hair pulling and his/her family circumstances. Developmental stages, maturity, and family situations all contribute to the overall impact that trichotillomania has on the child and the family. In the next chapter we will explore the emotional toll trichotillomania can have on parents.

3
Common Feelings and Reactions Parents Experience

This feels horrible!

Most parents who discover that their children are pulling their hair initially feel scared. It's unsettling at best to see your child engage in a behavior that seems so odd and so unfamiliar to you. In addition, the resulting bald spot draws unwanted attention to your child and ultimately to you. The unspoken reaction from others may be perceived as (in many cases accurately), "What in heavens name are you doing at home that is causing your child to pull out his/her hair?" or "You must be an awful parent!" Even if others aren't thinking this, very often moms and dads are thinking this about themselves. It feels absolutely awful. Nothing that you have been able to do has been successful, and the hair pulling just seems to be getting worse.

Parents frequently feel angry at their children for doing this to themselves and angry at themselves for being absolutely helpless. These feelings can also make parents feel lonely.

Most parents have difficulty talking about it to other people. After all, what are they going to think? "I already feel like the worst parent in the world. I don't need someone else telling me that." So many parents keep the information to themselves and feel isolated. Worst of all, parents can feel ashamed of their child for the way he/she looks. They find themselves wanting to cover the hair loss to avoid their own embarrassment and shame about how their child looks, even when the child does not really care. All of these feelings are normal and common reactions to dealing with a child who has trich. Before we try to cope with these feelings, let's try to understand a little more about trich and what you are dealing with.

I am so frustrated!

As stated in Chapter 1, trich is a complex behavior that manifests itself a little differently for each person. A trained psychologist or other mental health provider knows that it is valuable to evaluate a child's behavior completely before a comprehensive behavioral treatment plan can be formulated. But for many parents, it is hard to understand that the process of change takes time. Oftentimes, parents bring their child to therapy and want specific techniques up front, during the initial session. Some strategies can be offered at the onset, but a thorough evaluation is necessary before specific, tailored strategies can be offered. In other words, be patient. It is important for your child's therapist to develop a trusting relationship with your child and to fully understand how hair pulling works for him/her.

Getting your child ready to participate in treatment may take some time. As stated earlier, parents are often motivated for therapy, and the child is ambivalent at best. It can take several sessions of working with a child to get him/her to the point of readiness—and sometimes it takes longer. Have you ever been told that you should lose weight and not gone out the next day and started a program of weight loss? Have you ever joined a health club and not gone to work out there? Sometimes it takes weeks, months, or even years before one is at the point of saying, "OK, I am ready to do this." Understand that your child may not be at the point of readiness at the same time you are. Give your child time to get there. If your child is there, the treatment will be much more successful than if you are pushing the process.

All four case examples demonstrate parents who are more motivated for change than their children. As a result, they experience common pitfalls and make mistakes that happen all too often in the case of childhood and adolescent trich. Let's see how each of them proceeds along their course of treatment.

I can be patient, if she would just hurry up and change!

Ashley's parents decided to take her to the pediatrician to address her pulling while sucking her thumb. The doctor recommended that they ignore the behavior. Charles and Jane made every effort to ignore it. When Ashley sucked her thumb and pulled her hair, Jane got very upset. She didn't say anything directly, but she became visibly upset and sometimes cried. She would say, "You want your hair to grow nice and long so we can put it into a pretty ponytail, don't you?" or "Look at Dora the Explorer's pretty hair. You want your hair to look like that, right?" Since Jane was not commenting on the pulling, she thought that she was doing a good job at ignoring the behavior. However, Jane also became very upset and teary sometimes. At other times, she abruptly left the room to cry. Ashley was confused and upset. She didn't really understand why her mother was so sad, but she did know that she was the cause.

Charles was usually gone during work hours, thus he did not witness Ashley's daytime pulling. When he got home, he spent a lot of time trying to comfort Jane. Charles was very frustrated. When he put Ashley to bed, he simply took her hands down whenever they crept up to her head. This frustrated Ashley. She cried and sometimes tried to hit Charles when he took her hand down. He tried putting socks on her hands, but she promptly took them off. Charles became aggravated, and he eventually avoided tucking Ashley into bed altogether.

Charles and Jane thought, what a mess! This ignoring is definitely not working! Well, we agree that their attempts were not working, but Charles and Jane also were not ignoring the behavior. Just the opposite, they were paying close attention to the behavior and had VERY strong reactions.

All children, particularly young children, are exquisitely tuned in to their parents' reactions to them. Children find it extremely interesting to watch their parents react as a result of their behavior. This makes them feel very powerful. Sometimes this is fun for them, and other times it's confusing. Often children don't want that much power. However, they do want attention. And if they can't get positive attention, any attention will do. In addition, hair pulling felt good to Ashley—most of the time she was pulling simply because it soothed her. She was confused to see her parents get upset when she was just doing something that felt good.

It is extremely difficult to ignore an unwanted behavior in your child. Ignoring behavior means not responding to it AT ALL. No comments about hair, no comments about other people's hair, no attempts to stop the behavior—nothing. For many parents (if not most) ignoring behavior is almost impossible. If you feel that you cannot truly ignore it, don't even try—ask for another suggestion.

Patience with yourself and your child is key at this stage. You must be patient when deciding which suggestions make sense for you and your family, as well as when trying out some different intervention ideas. Trying something and ultimately determining that it won't work for you is as important as finding out what does work. For Charles and Jane, they can confidently state that ignoring is not a workable strategy. If the pediatrician has nothing more to offer, they need to seek guidance elsewhere.

The blame game

Stu and Karen, the parents of second grade Sarah, took her to see a dermatologist as they thought that perhaps a skin disorder was causing her eyelashes and eyebrows to fall out. The dermatologist determined that the hairs had been plucked and that trichotillomania, not alopecia, was the diagnosis. The family was referred to a therapist who knew about behavior therapy, but had never heard about trichotillomania.

At first, Sarah did not even want to talk to the therapist. She was completely unwilling to discuss hair or hair pulling, still adamantly denying that she pulled. The therapist was patient with her, but Stu and Karen were growing impatient. They wanted to see results quickly and were worried that her friends would start to notice the hair-loss and ask questions. Karen inadvertently made Sarah feel guilty by saying things like "We are paying a lot of money for this therapy, you need to work harder!" Sarah began to shut down and not trust her parents the way she used to, for fear of getting in trouble. Stu, thinking he was being encouraging, commented about her lashes and brows, stating that, "You look so much prettier with your eyelashes and eyebrows, why don't you want them to grow back?" What he did not realize is that she desperately wanted them to grow back.

Sarah began to feel she must be ugly because her parents kept telling her she was prettier with her lashes and brows, and she had not had these in months. She eventually began to withdraw from friends at school, fearing that they too would judge her harshly for her lack of lashes and brows. Sarah felt misunderstood, blamed, pushed, and frustrated. The common mistake that Stu and Karen made here is called BLAMING. Have you ever blamed your child for some behavior, even though it was beyond his/her control? The mistake is unfortunately very common and can lead to shame and humiliation on the part of the sufferer.

It is common for parents to feel both frustrated and out of control in response to their child's trich, mainly because it IS out of parents' control. Moreover, it is difficult at best for a child to control pulling behavior—but it IS possible. Parents blame themselves and, at times, inadvertently pass that blame along to their child. But what is a parent to do? Ignoring doesn't work. Pointing out the obvious benefits to having hair doesn't work. What can be done?

It's the hair police!

Hannah was more than willing to attend sessions with the school counselor each week. Her counselor had purchased a workbook for teens with trich and she was going through the workbook with Hannah each week. Hannah was becoming concerned about her hair loss and was willing to do anything to grow it back. Interestingly, when the counselor gave her homework to do on her own, Hannah was inconsistent. She had some good weeks and some bad weeks with regard to pulling, which was confusing to Hannah, her counselor, and her parents. When her hair started to grow back, her parents praised the hair growth and rewarded her for her success. At other times, however, this "success" would be immediately followed by a setback. Peggy and Bob wondered what was wrong with Hannah and why she could not be consistent with the treatment. The more setbacks she had, the more difficult it was to re-establish her motivation.

Soon, Hannah began to feel that familiar sense of helplessness and started to give up. Unfortunately her counselor, with limited experience treating trich, also began to feel helpless. She requested fewer visits with Hannah, and eventually they stopped the visits altogether. Hannah began to believe that she would never get control over her pulling and, as a result, she would never be acceptable to others.

Without intending to do so, Hannah's parents had become the "hair police" and had come only to see "hair" or "no hair" as a measure of her success as a person. When Hannah came home from school, her parents closely inspected her hair to see if she had pulled any. They thought they were being subtle and that Hannah didn't notice, but she did. She saw the disappointment and sometimes anger in their faces when they noticed that she had pulled at school. As a result, she began to dread coming home because she did not want to disappoint them. Good grades on a report card were somehow not as wonderful because they were overshadowed by a relapse. Hannah began to believe that her success with trich was all that mattered. She began to believe that unless she mastered not pulling, she would not be able to live a happy life.

We call this mistake POLICING. When parents become so focused on the presence or absence of hair, they literally "police" their child daily on their hair status. In addition, parents often feel that they have no other option than to be punitive around hair pulling issues. Some punish their child for pulling or try to get his/her attention by pointing out the hair loss. Others question whether or not the child really wants to stop.

While it is normal for parents to go through a period of frustration and panic in the beginning, POLICING can make children feel confused and "down" on themselves. You love your child and want the best for him/her. The last thing you want is to see your child teased or humiliated on the playground for having no eyelashes or a bald spot on his/her head.

However, what we have seen clinically is that a punitive approach does not work; in fact, it can contribute to feelings of frustration and promote both shame and worthlessness, which exacerbate the problem.

The most powerful feedback that children can get is from their peers. However, children younger than 11 years old often do not care what their hair looks like, so parental or peer feedback usually gets little to no desirable response. When they reach middle school, however, peers may start to tease and make comments. Sometimes this is the motivator that can help them become ready to work on their hair pulling.

So what are parents to do? We recommend that you focus on other characteristics of your child, rather than on hair pulling. We realize that this can be very hard to do! It may help to sit down and make a list of all of the positive aspects of your child. Make sure that each day you are commenting, noticing, and encouraging several of these wonderful traits. It is common for parents to only see "hair or no hair," and to forget about all of the many talents and attributes of their child. When you are acting as the "hair police," your child learns that hair growth is the most important part of him/her, which can lead to feelings of not measuring up, low self-esteem, and poor confidence.

Too much focus: Hair today, gone tomorrow

Hayden ended up in therapy as well for trich. His pulling had been going on for some time and had become so severe that he had developed a large bald spot on his head. Because the therapist who saw him had little experience in treating trich, she was alarmed with his level of hair loss. She immediately referred him to a psychiatrist who put him on anti-depressant medication. Most or all of the focus of treatment with the psychiatrist turned toward his pulling. Why was he still pulling despite the medication? Several times the medication was increased and changed. Still, no change in hair pulling occurred.

Ellen took Hayden to his session when he was staying with her and his dad took him if he was at his house. Both parents were defensive about how Hayden did at their respective houses, downplaying the marital discord that had become so prevalent. Hayden's hair pulling became the focus of all of his treatment. Even when the psychiatrist tried to turn the focus onto other issues, such as the divorce, they shifted it back to his trich. Hayden continued pulling. Ellen and Fred continued to nag Hayden about his pulling and to pressure him to stop. The mistake that Ellen and Fred make here is called TOO MUCH

FOCUS on trich, at the expense of other circumstances, qualities, and unique attributes.

All four of these common responses— IMPATIENCE,
BLAMING, POLICING, and TOO MUCH FOCUS—are widespread for parents. In fact, most well meaning, good parents
have had one, some, or all of these experiences at some point
in time. Although it is important to recognize these reactions
in yourself, it is equally important to move forward. Instead of
berating yourself for the past, move forward into recognizing
and understanding your own feelings, then learn how you can
react differently in the future.

How do you do this? Understanding how you feel will
be an important first step. In addition, it will be helpful to
understand hair pulling behavior in a different way—how hair
pulling is meeting a need for your child. This new perspective
on the behavior can help lead to compassion and can alleviate
the fear that all parents experience when they discover their
child's hair pulling. In the next chapter, we will explore how
hair pulling started for each of these children and how a better
understanding of trichotillomania in general helped each parent cope with their own fears and reactions.

4
Understanding Leads
to Compassion

Trichotillomania as a soothing behavior

Ashley

After attending a regional workshop about trichotillomania, Jane obtained some important information about how
to understand Ashley. She began to observe Ashley's behavior
to try to understand it. Through watching Ashley's hair pulling
patterns and talking with her gently about her pulling, Charles
and Jane were able to understand that for Ashley, hair pulling
was her way of soothing herself to sleep. She cuddled up with
her blanket, placed her thumb in her mouth, and started to twirl.
The pulling really was more of a side effect of the twirling,
rather than a purposeful behavior. Charles and Jane noticed
that pulling happened more frequently when Ashley was overtired and had been particularly busy that day. On days that
were less "hurried," she pulled less. This information alone
helped Charles and Jane with their reactions to Ashley's pulling. First, they realized that her pulling fell into a pattern and

that as parents, they had some control over the situation. Second, they felt like they understood Ashley's attempts to calm herself when she was overly tired.   Most importantly, they learned PATIENCE with Ashley. Instead of simply reacting to her hair pulling, Charles and Jane became careful observers of their daughter's behavior.

Jane recalled that when she was tired or overworked during the day, she took a hot bath at night to soothe her and help her settle down. Was this really any different? Charles recalled that as a child he had a soft toy that he rubbed with his fingers (until it literally disintegrated) to help him calm himself. Both Charles and Jane were able to connect with Ashley's behavior as "adaptive" and therefore began to problem-solve, rather than feel helpless.

Behavior that begins as adaptive can become a habit

Sarah

Stu and Karen finally took Sarah to a trained therapist who was able to talk to Sarah about her pulling. Sarah was able to open up with the therapist because she seemed to know what she was talking about—she seemed to understand her.

Sarah reported that she began pulling out her eyelashes several months before when her allergies had gotten bad in the spring. She had experienced intense itching in her eyes which led to pulling out her eyelashes to relieve the itching. Soon, the pulling became more of a habit, especially after the allergies had resolved. The pulling eventually moved to her eyebrows as well.

Sarah told the therapist that presently the pulling happened mostly at school, usually during the afternoon classes. She described feeling bored and sometimes confused in school and that pulling gave her something to do. Sometimes she lined up the hairs on her desk and compared them. Other times she softly rubbed the hairs along her lips because it felt "tingly" to her and helped her to relax.

Sarah's therapist was able to explain to Stu and Karen how Sarah was using hair pulling as a way of coping. When Sarah was finally able to talk to her parents about her pulling, they were more able to understand her, instead of judge her. Stu and Karen were beginning the process of ACCEPTING Sarah as having trichotillomania. This does not necessarily mean that they like it, but that they accept that it is a part of their lives and that it is, in part, how Sarah gets her needs met. They were starting to understand their daughter and the healing was about to begin.

Lifting the shame

Hannah

Peggy and Bob finally found some answers at a TLC retreat. They took Hannah to a weekend experience where trained professionals were available to help them understand Hannah and learn about her trich. During the weekend, Hannah learned and eventually disclosed that her pulling was fairly complex. She was first drawn to pulling her pubic hair at the onset of puberty. Her pubic hair was much more coarse and thick than other hair on her body, and she noticed that her pubic hairs had large bulbs attached to them. She began by sitting on the toilet and spent 30-45 minutes at a time pulling. It started more as a fascination and later turned into a problem.

Feeling mortified to tell her parents that she even had pubic hair, much less that she was pulling it out, she tried to stop. As a result, she moved to pulling her scalp hair. She reasoned that she had much more scalp hair and that she could never pull enough to create a problem. These hairs, she explained, were less coarse and had smaller bulbs, but felt really good to pull. She sat in front of the mirror in the morning and pulled any ones that were darker, sticking out, or looked out of place. Before long, she could talk herself into pulling any of them. It had become such a part of her morning grooming ritual that she could not imagine stopping.

Eventually, Hannah's hair pulling had become more than just a grooming ritual. Over the months, she had started to pull when she was worried about peer-related issues. Several girls at school were being mean to her, and the pulling had helped her to "think through" the situation and to "feel better." Now, her pulling was happening during studying and during TV watching, as well as during times of emotional turmoil.

Peggy and Bob were floored. They could not believe how honest Hannah was about her pulling just from attending a retreat. The experience of being around other teens had helped her to feel less ashamed about her pulling. They noticed that she was acting more like her old self, laughing, smiling, and seemingly happier. In addition to Hannah changing, Peggy and Bob noticed changes within themselves over the course of the weekend.

Peggy noticed that she also felt less shame about Hannah's pulling. Talking with other parents who were "in the same boat" helped Peggy to realize that Hannah's pulling did not make her "weird" or "destined for a life of misery," but was simply something that she did to help her cope in difficult situations. In fact, Peggy was able to talk to several adults who had pulled as children or teens. These people had learned how to manage their pulling and were, much to her delight, normal, lovely adults. Peggy began to feel more optimistic for Hannah. She felt herself move through her grief and sadness into acceptance and hope. Most importantly, Peggy began to refocus. She began to remember all of the wonderful aspects of Hannah: her humor, her independence, her outgoing personality, her compassion for others—things that she had forgotten due to her narrow focus on hair pulling.

Bob had a curative experience through attending the retreat, however in a little different way. Bob had not experienced shame or fear in response to Hannah's pulling, but he did experience anger. He could not see why she could not just quit. Why was it so hard for her to stop? He took a black and white approach and wanted to punish her for pulling. Moreover, he witnessed how Hannah's pulling negatively impacted Peggy, and this made him even angrier.

Through talking with other parents and professionals at the retreat, he realized that hair pulling was not under Hannah's control, that stopping was not so simple. He also came to understand that his anger toward Hannah was not helping; in fact, it was actually hurting her. Bob learned other strategies for coping with his emotions, as well as ways to help Hannah that did not involve blame, punishment, or attempts to control her behavior. He learned how to avoid power struggles with his daughter and how to engage her in productive, fruitful conversation. As a result, Bob felt less helpless and more hopeful about the future.

Hair pulling in context

Hayden

Hayden stopped seeing the psychiatrist and was eventually taken off of the medications. After finding a behavior therapy group in their area with trained therapists who had much experience in treating individuals with trich, Ellen and Fred began to get some answers. They learned that medications were not the first line of intervention for trich and that there was no medication that consistently worked for reducing hair pulling symptoms. The new therapist was able to explain that Hayden's trich may or may not have had anything to do with his parents' divorce, but it had become the focus of much of the parental discord and a way for him to deal with unpleasant feelings.

What Ellen and Fred learned through family therapy sessions was that Hayden pulled to relieve his stress and soothe himself in a variety of emotionally difficult situations. Academic pressure, boredom, and intense sensory experiences while playing with the hair all perpetuated his pulling. He was soothing himself on many different levels: physical, emotional, and psychological.

Once the therapy began to broaden to family-based issues and Ellen and Fred learned appropriate communication skills with each other, as well as with their children, things started to improve. As their other children were included in the treatment, the therapist began to identify a multitude of coping strategies that each of their children had adopted to deal with their situations. By looking at the trich in the context of the larger family system, Ellen and Fred were able to have compassion for all of their children and to learn more appropriate ways of intervening and communicating.

As these case studies have demonstrated, negative reactions to pulling are natural and common. However, through understanding your child's unique situation you will develop compassion for your child, and ultimately you will be ready to intervene in a proactive and helpful manner. In the next chapter, we will look specifically at what you can do to assist your child in his/her journey to recovery.

5
OK...What Do I Do Now?

Strategies for change

What strategies would one use for success? A reasonable question, but difficult to answer. The most important thing is, are you ready to take the next step in helping your child? If you are the parent of a very young child, an elementary school age child, or a child in middle school, you will need time, energy, and support. As is true with any childhood problem, the parents are always somewhat involved in the process of managing the issue. Sometimes the involvement is all-encompassing, as with very young children. At other times, parents are involved in the organization and oversight. Most of the time, the parents are lead cheerleaders, major support systems, and trouble-shooters. Just thinking about it can be overwhelming! Given all of these important roles, do you have the time and energy to devote to this cause?   Is this the right time for your family? Is this the right time for you? If so, it is just as important for you to commit to this process as it is for your child. Many times, parents have trouble staying consistent with the strategies suggested and end up dropping the ball for very good reasons. Parents have numerous responsibilities, family obligations, children's activities, and work-related tasks to tend to daily. It's important to take all of this into consideration when deciding if this is the right time to start working on hair pulling.

So take care of yourself. Do you have the emotional resources necessary to embark on this process? If not, what do you need? How can you get support? Make sure that you have some time for yourself that is recreational. Develop some good "hobbies" that are stress relieving: reading, exercise, time with friends, sports, card games, etc. In sum, first make sure you are ready and able to make a commitment to helping your child in a calm and responsible fashion and second, take steps to care for yourself along the way. This is a wonderful opportunity to become a role-model for your child about how to approach a difficult problem.

We want our children to be able take a step back, gather the resources necessary to address their problems, and garner support to be successful. As parents, we need to do this first. Demonstrate for your child how it is done. Recognize your needs and try to meet those needs to the best of your ability. Modeling can be an important tool to help your child, and in the process, help yourself.

In addition to evaluating your own readiness to embark on this journey, you also want to make sure that the family is prepared for this endeavor. It may mean that there is more time and energy devoted to one child. If your family is already experiencing stress (due to marital difficulties, another child with robust issues in need of attention, or communication difficulties frequently leading to arguments), you will need to attend to these issues first. Although these family dynamics may not have caused the hair pulling, they will undoubtedly contribute to it at some point. It is normal for families to experience stress (moving to a new area, a death in the family, divorce, etc.) and challenges. In response to stress, families must develop good coping skills to function well. If your family is experiencing acute challenges, you may want to address these first, before devoting yourselves to working on hair pulling. Changing behavior can be a time consuming task that requires focus and energy. By addressing pressing or acute matters first, your family may be more ready and better equipped to handle the challenges that trichotillomania may present.

How do you hurry up and wait?

O

Ashley

While watching Ashley's patterns and learning about her pulling behavior, Charles and Jane decided to take a step back and do some research about trichotillomania in very young children, or what has been referred to as "baby trich." This process took patience. Each day, Charles and Jane gave themselves a web site or article to read. At the end of the day, they shared with each other what they had learned. After a few weeks, they became more informed about trichotillomania in general, and about "baby trich" specifically. Just reading about other families dealing with similar problems helped them feel validated and hopeful. They began to believe that this situation could improve.

Charles and Jane decided to talk with someone who had treated a number of children with pre-school hair pulling, even though that professional did not live in their state. They had several hour-long phone consults with this therapist to learn what she knew and to tell her what they had observed in Ashley. The therapist remarked at how wonderfully they were doing in observing and watching—and being patient. She told Jane that patience with Ashley would eventually lead Ashley to feel calm, safe, and nurtured. Gathering information from a very knowledgeable source made them feel much better.

Jane understood that the strategies would be mostly her responsibility and that she needed to be emotionally prepared. Jane decided to take a yoga class with a friend. This gave her some much needed time to herself doing something that she loved, and provided her with good exercise three times a week. Jane also decided to join a mom's group. This allowed her some adult interaction and Ashley some other kids to play with. Even though the other moms were not coping with their children pulling hair, they were all struggling with some aspect of parenting. This made Jane feel more like a "normal parent."

Jane realized that gathering information, finding time for herself, and developing a support system all helped her become ready to work on Ashley's pulling. Being PATIENT with herself really made a huge difference in Jane's outlook. It also helped her become more patient with Ashley. Things would not change over night, or even in a week, but Jane was feeling better in general and could see that given time and patience, change would come. Do you find yourself becoming IMPATIENT with your child? Have you ever snapped at him/her for pulling or even fiddling with hair? If so, try to exercise

PATIENCE with your child. Take deep breaths, walk away, take a break, or make a neutral statement or no statement at all when you want to snap.

When things are better, I'll accept them

Sarah

Stu and Karen decided to speak with someone who knew about trichotillomania. They gathered reading material and talked about their feelings. Karen realized that she was embarrassed by Sarah's appearance. In addition, Karen felt that she had failed her daughter as a mother and blamed herself for Sarah's pulling. These feelings of blame and embarrassment deeply affected how Karen felt about herself as a mother, and how she felt about Sarah. Karen realized that she also "blamed" Sarah for making her feel terrible.

Once Karen understood her feelings, it was easier (not easy, though) to examine them. Over time, Karen began to ACCEPT that she was not to blame for Sarah's pulling and that Sarah could work on the hair pulling when she was ready. She learned that ACCEPTING Sarah's hair pulling did not mean that she condoned it or that she was resigning herself to "allow" it to continue. It simply meant that hair pulling was a part of how Sarah copes. She was able to understand trich as a part of who Sarah was, not a trait to establish blame for.

If Karen could help, she would be happy to, but Sarah needed to be willing to work on managing her pulling on her own. It would never have occurred to Karen that she might need some help when dealing with Sarah's hair pulling, but once she accepted that it was neither her fault nor Sarah's, it became much less tense around the house.

Sarah soon started talking to her parents again like she used to, because her parents had stopped saying negative things about her hair. An important breakthrough happened one day when Sarah came home from school after a particularly boring math class where she pulled out all of her eyelashes again. When she got home she braced herself for the inspection and the usual "guilt trip"—except it didn't happen. Karen sat down and asked Sarah about her day. Karen listened as Sarah complained about math. Then Karen got up from her seat and prepared a special snack for Sarah because she had a tough day in math. Nothing was said about Sarah's hair, the money they were spending on therapy, or whether or not Sarah was really ready to stop pulling. Sarah was so relieved that she almost cried. This allowed Sarah to slowly open up and helped Karen to feel closer to her. Their relationship improved and they became more of a team, rather than behaving as if they were opponents.

Sarah began to ACCEPT herself. Karen began to ACCEPT Sarah. And the whole family ACCEPTED that trichotillomania was part of the family—for the moment. It didn't mean that anyone was a bad child or a bad parent, just that this was what was happening in the family for the time being. Have you accepted trich as a part of your child's life? Do you find yourself just wishing that it would go away? Remember, ACCEPTING does not mean "condoning" hair pulling, or even liking it; it means simply acknowledging that it IS in your life.

Releasing, not policing

Hannah

Peggy and Bob were exhausted being the hair police. They hated doing this and Hannah hated it even more. The TLC weekend retreat helped Peggy to understand Hannah and why she was pulling, and to have compassion for her as a developing adolescent. Adolescence is hard enough! Peggy started to talk to Hannah about her feelings, not her hair. At the retreat, Peggy learned that she wasn't helping by POLIC-

ING, that she needed to stop. This was very hard for Peggy. She started turning to Bob for support and made a plan to RE-LEASE, NOT POLICE.

Peggy took deep breaths every time she wanted to comment on hair or to tell Hannah to "get your hand out of your hair." The breathing helped Peggy to relax a bit. She made a point of not saying anything about hair for one day. Then Peggy added another day to her goal and so on. Soon, Peggy was able to go for long periods without saying anything about Hannah's hair, and her deep breathing allowed her to RELEASE tension around hair pulling issues. Eventually, Peggy noticed that as she was changing, so was Hannah. Hannah began to relax.

Although Hannah continued to pull her hair, she and Peggy began to talk about a variety of things, like other mothers and daughters. Once Hannah felt more comfortable, she and Peggy started to talk about the hair pulling in a different way. Peggy asked Hannah if there was anything she could do to help with her trich. Hannah was surprised and delighted by her mother's view of her as the expert. Hannah suggested a system to help her remember to use her strategies. Rather than nagging, Hannah came up with a secret word that Peggy was to use when Hannah was pulling or her hand was in her hair. This code word made Hannah laugh, so when she heard her mother say it, she was able to use her strategies right away.

Peggy realized what a difference it made to be able to RELEASE and not POLICE. Her relationship improved with her daughter and Peggy felt much better about herself. Do you find yourself POLICING your child and his/her hair? Do you catch yourself inspecting hair growth, nagging when you see hair play, or responding negatively to obvious pulling? If so, try to police yourself. Make a commitment to let go of or RELEASE your desire to control your child—you will be surprised by the results!

Changing focus

Hayden

Through intensive family therapy and individual treatment for trich, Hayden stopped pulling. He turned his energy toward sports and became involved in basketball. His father played basketball in high school as well, so this was a nice activity which allowed them to spend time together practicing and talking. Hayden stopped blaming his father for leaving the family and eventually their relationship healed. Ellen and Fred learned that the most important people in their lives were their children, and together they decided to put them first. They learned not to blame each other when things went wrong and stopped putting the children in the middle of their relationship. Most importantly, they learned to focus on Hayden's accomplishments, not his struggles—especially not his trich. All too often parents become too FOCUSED on hair and hair pulling issues, much to the detriment of their child's development and self-esteem. The outcome of this SHIFT IN FOCUS was that Hayden improved dramatically in basketball and was recognized as an outstanding player by the school. Hayden's self-esteem grew and the need to soothe himself through hair pulling decreased.

Where is your focus with regard to your child? Do you tend to focus too much on issues surrounding hair? Have you neglected important aspects of your child that need attention? If so, SHIFT YOUR FOCUS to these other areas and see what happens.

Although each child is pulling his or her hair, every child has a distinct experience. In addition, hair pulling is approached differently by parents and professionals depending upon the child's age and stage of development. In the next chapter we will explore trichotillomania from infancy through high school.

6
Different Ages and Different Stages of Trich

Baby trich

Trichotillomania looks different during different ages and developmental stages. It is important to understand your child's developmental stage in order to adequately understand his/her hair pulling. For example, some people believe that hair pulling under the age of five is not trichotillomania exactly, but rather a phenomenon known as "baby trich." With baby trich, children do not always develop full blown trichotillomania when they get older and may even outgrow it. A common recommendation at this age is to ignore the behavior and it will go away on its own. What if it doesn't go away? What if you can't ignore it?

We have learned that early intervention can be enormously successful and that children who have learned to manage hair pulling at an early age are not likely to develop it later. This suggests that the "wait and see if she grows out of it" approach is not always the best.

So what does hair pulling look like for the very young? Very young children who engage in hair pulling often combine it with other self-soothing behaviors. For these youngsters, hair pulling usually occurs when the child is sucking his/her thumb. In addition, most children pull when they are tired or slightly bored. These times usually include lying down for a nap, riding in the car, going to sleep for the night, or waking up. Other times might include listening to a story or watching TV. Some children at this age do not suck their thumbs, but do pull their hair. However, for these kids, the situations usually mirror those of children who suck their thumbs.

Children at this age are learning new things every minute of every day. This is a wonderful time to introduce how to be tired or cranky without pulling one's hair. Also, it's an excellent opportunity to introduce alternate self-soothing techniques. Most children at this age are very interested in exploring their world. They are limited, however, in how they explore it. Children use their senses to discover things at this age. Therefore, examining the texture of something, how something feels in the mouth or rubbed on the face or head, is very important. It is also an opportunity to soothe one's self, because these different things feel good. Remember what feels good to a baby or toddler does not always feel good to an adult. Also, what feels good to one person may not feel good to someone else. Don't assume that because hair pulling hurts to you that it also hurts to your child. Very often this behavior feels good, is soothing, and provides some interest for your child.

If your young child is pulling hair, you may be wondering, "How does this apply to me and my child? What am I supposed to do?" First, you will need to observe when your child is likely to engage in hair pulling. As mentioned earlier, usually these times include, but are not limited to, when your child is tired, going to sleep or waking up, listening to a story or book, watching TV or a video, and in the car. If your child sucks his/her thumb, as Ashley does, this can contribute to or trigger hair pulling as well.

For all children, sensory stimulation is important. Unlike older children, however, little children do not have the cognitive capability to work on modifying their own behavior. Therefore, blocking the ability to pull is an important first step. Have your child wear a very pretty, light-weight pair of gloves during times when he/she is more likely to pull. These gloves are usually found around Easter time or are those worn by children in weddings. Other possibilities are gloves with finger puppets or sock puppets. Your child can wear the gloves at night and receive a sticker or small reward in the morning for waking up with the gloves on. It's important to use fun, appealing, and light weight gloves or sock puppets. Children usually intensely dislike wearing winter gloves because they are hot. Comfortable, appealing gloves are usually more palatable. In addition, giving a little reward for compliance usually helps the child feel good about the process.

Sensory input is also important. Children need to have lots of sensory input. Having you or your child brush his/her hair can feel really good. (Children should not run their hands through their hair, however. It's too tempting!) Introduce interesting brushes or combs to your child to see what he or she prefers. Also, provide highly tactile toys such as pipe cleaners and inside out balls in "trigger" situations to allow your child to address any tactile needs.

Just like with any behavior at this age, you are shaping your child's new behavior by encouraging alternative activities rather than hair pulling. Remember that rewards will be very helpful at this stage. Stickers or little "grab bag" toys are highly appealing and keep children motivated behavior change. Nothing is more rewarding, however, than mommy and/or daddy clapping, smiling, and hugging them. All rewards should be given with this type of enthusiasm. Please remember that you are rewarding the use of strategies (wearing gloves, using tactile toys, playing with finger puppets), not hair growth.

This type of program is often very hard to do on your own. It usually requires support and regular adjustments to be successful. Working with a therapist who specializes in dealing with small children might be very helpful. If this is not possible, working with an occupational therapist who has experience with small children may be a good alternative.

In order to help very young children with hair pulling, we must understand their hair pulling behavior, what need it is addressing, when the behavior is more likely to occur, and what sensations the child is gaining from the behavior. As you may recall, Jane noticed that Ashley pulled more on days that were long or when she was overtired. This information gave Jane and her husband some idea of how to change situations to make them less high risk. They decided to limit activities during the day to avoid Ashley becoming overtired, provided light gloves for her at night, and made sure that she had plenty of soothing down time in the evening to wind down the day.

During treatment, your therapist will develop a behavioral plan and will provide strategies to help your child develop alternate ways to cope with emotional and sensory experiences. This is a delicate process. Your therapist may help you to make this process fun, otherwise situations can deteriorate quickly into a battle of wills, which you will always lose. As mentioned previously, it is useful that you have the energy, enthusiasm, and support to be able to work on this behavior. It is equally important to know your child's temperament and stage of development in order to ensure a successful experience.

Children at these ages vary widely in their development. Some children are pre-verbal and others are talking up a storm. Some children are headstrong and want to do everything themselves, while others are agreeable and compliant. It's important to really know your child and what stage he/she is in. If your child is in the "no" stage, you may want to wait a few months to start introducing strategies to help with hair pulling. If your child is just beginning potty training, now may not be a good time to introduce yet another way to control your child's behavior.

The good news is, children go through these stages pretty quickly. If you wait a few weeks, or sometimes a month or two, children are on to other things. It's never going to be ideal, but there are some stages such as potty training, moving, or introducing a new sibling that consistently are more difficult than others.

The elementary school-age child

For children under the age of 11, trichotillomania affects as many boys as it does girls. After the age of 11, girls outnumber boys with trich 9 to 1. As far as we know, there have not been any long-term studies on children with baby trich to determine for sure whether or not these children do indeed "grow out of it" or if they do, in fact, develop trich later in life. The usual course of the disorder is to wax and wane over many years before taking solid hold. What is common among younger children is that oftentimes they are very confused about their pulling. They experience such pleasure with pulling, yet they sense their parents' unhappiness with the behavior.

Children younger than 11 years are typically less concerned with hair loss than those who have reached middle school and all the associated peer pressures. As a result, treatment may consist of providing rewards to encourage the use of strategies. Children this young may not work for hair growth, but oftentimes they will work for a reward.

Children at this stage (5-11 years) need more than anything to feel loved and accepted. Anxiety is common in children in the elementary school years, and feeling unaccepted, punished, shamed, or humiliated can lead to fear, confusion, insecurity, and anxiety. If your child is in these middle years, make it very clear that your love and acceptance is unconditional. This means that whether or not your child is pulling out hair, completely bald, or lacking eyelashes or eyebrows, he/she is still a valued, loved, and cherished individual.

Many times you will be biting your tongue when you want to comment or "help." Educate your child about trich— let him/her know that hair pulling is just a small part of who he/she is, and that you love the whole package. Help yourself begin to accept trich as a way of coping with difficult situations. Make sure you (or a therapist) are teaching your child alternate coping strategies for these situations.

Acceptance requires you to work on your feelings of frustration and shame. You must get your feelings in check before you can expect your child to do the same. Children absolutely need to feel like their parents are in control and can handle all kinds of situations. When a child suspects that her parents feel out of control or, worse, that she is in control of how her parents feel, she may become frightened. If your reactions to your child resemble crying, begging, terror, rage, blaming, hysteria, or other intense emotional turmoil, your child is in control. If your reaction is empathy, i.e., "I am sorry you had a

hard day, do you want to talk about it?" instead of "I can't believe how much you pulled!" or "This is horrible—people are
going to think you are weird and you won't have any friends!"
your child will feel safe and that you can handle yourself and
the situation.

If anxiety is present during this time in the form of fears,
phobias, obsessions, compulsions, or avoidance, be careful not
to attribute this solely to trich. It is not unusual for children to
have some anxiety during these elementary years. Children at
this age need to feel safe within the structure of the home and
to have clear expectations and consequences. Loose structure
or vague expectations within the family can lead children to
feel anxious and sometimes to act out. The resultant anxiety is
completely separate from trich. Common mistakes that parents
make in reaction to trich are either to further loosen the home
structure or to become overly strict, yet unpredictable with
regard to expectations and consequences. These approaches
only make matters worse and more confusing for the child and
can lead to more insecurity and anxiety—and more pulling!

In the late elementary and middle school years, children
are fragile with regard to self-esteem. Help your budding adolescent feel pride and accomplishment for things that he/she is
good at doing. Try not to focus on hair pulling, but rather focus

on sports, art, academics, theater, writing, hobbies, etc. If your child has not yet found a particular area of strength, provide opportunities to experience a variety of new activities. Be supportive of different ideas and praise your child for trying new things, even if they are a struggle.

The middle school-age child

Middle school is a time of tremendous change for children, both physically and emotionally. In treatment, the types of strategies selected and level of parent involvement will depend largely upon the child's temperament, maturity, and relationship with the parent. Some early adolescents are happy to have their parents involved in helping them. Other children at this age begin to feel the need for greater independence from their parents. You, with the help of a therapist, should determine how much involvement is going to be helpful to your child, and also when to back off. Trained professionals assist children in talking about feelings and can help parents feel more comfortable taking less of a leadership role.

Middle school is typically the time when children begin to experience teasing from their peers as a result of their hair pulling and for other, non-trich reasons. Your role is to support your child, so that he/she is able to cope with these unfortunate interactions. Instead of using teasing as a way for you to make your point about why he/she should stop pulling, give your child the words that are needed to cope with these encounters. For example, Peggy and Bob taught Hannah to how to respond to peers who asked her "What happened to your hair?" with "I have trichotillomania, go look it up!" Hannah reported that other kids were so confused that they just walked away and eventually left her alone. She thought it was funny that she knew a word that other kids did not know, much less how to spell! Middle school is hard enough on kids, but having trich can make it almost unbearable. It is helpful to find ways to make having trich more tolerable for your child.

Sometimes parents need to intervene at the school to educate the faculty and administration about hair pulling or to make school personnel aware of brutality that may be going on toward their child. Educational literature to address school-related issues can be obtained through the TLC at www.trich.org.

Many times we recommend that a child wear a hat at school, if this is a common pulling place for him/her. Because most schools prohibit the wearing of hats, the school administration will have to be consulted and give permission for this to occur. In any event, your middle school child may need the extra assistance of a therapist to negotiate this difficult period. Provide this opportunity if your child is receptive, and keep your focus on what is truly important, your child's self-esteem.

The high school-age child

High school years bring unique challenges. Teenagers can be defiant and angry just by nature—then you add trich to the picture, and whew!   A great challenge that parents of adolescents face is managing their children's unpleasant behaviors without damaging the relationship. First, you need to understand that the struggle for independence in adolescence (the back talk, the disregard of rules, the pushing of limits) is a normal part of the "individuation" process. Individuation describes the process by which adolescents become increasingly independent from their parents in an attempt to discover who they are as separate people from their parents. Adolescents do this in a variety of ways, i.e., changing hair color, disregarding rules, slacking off of academics, becoming sexually active, or experimenting with alcohol and drugs. While the "limit testing" is somewhat normal, it is your responsibility to be vigilant to adolescent behavior, i.e., know what your child is up to, and set appropriate expectations and consequences. As if this isn't enough, adding trich to the equation can really create a mess!

The most common mistake that we see parents of adolescents make is to allow hair pulling to become a point of contention with their children—another battle in the war of adolescence. If your child knows that hair pulling will absolutely send you over the edge, guess what that child is going to do when mad at you? Adolescents know exactly what is going to punish you and they are likely to do it. Sometimes parents avoid doling out punishment for misbehavior because they are afraid it will lead to increased pulling. This is very dangerous as it allows the adolescent to be in control and not suffer necessary consequences to poor behavior. Do not allow the fear of hair pulling to prevent you from giving appropriate and deserved consequences.

If trich has become a way for your child to "get back at you," this can change, but it will take effort on your part. First, you must stop reacting to the hair pulling, no matter how obvious and extreme it is. Let your child know, through your lack of reaction, that the pulling only hurts the child, not you. Eventually, your child will turn to other strategies for "winning" the battle against you.

In sum, not only is hair pulling unique at each age and

stage of development, but so is parenting. Your role as a parent changes as your child does and so does your role as an advocate to help your child manage hair pulling. Being a good advocate requires a delicate balance of support, compassion, and knowledge. In the next chapter, we will help you understand exactly what you need to know when considering treatment for trichotillomania.

7
The Nuts and Bolts of Treatment

What to know

What is important to know about treatment for trich? Is it all the same? Are some treatments better than others? As scientists, we know that we must look to research to see what types of interventions have been proven to work with real people in the real world. The types of interventions for behavior change that have been effective in scientific studies are those that involve behavioral analysis (understanding the behavior), teaching specific coping strategies, and a long-term commitment to and management of behavioral change.

Before we describe the behavioral treatment for trich, it is important to talk about medications. Parents frequently ask about medicine because some want a "magic bullet" to cure their child, while others have been steered in this direction by a medical professional and are concerned about medicating their young child. Both issues are common and valid. Scientific investigations show that no medication works well for everyone. Several studies indicate improvement with medications for some people, but oftentimes the improvement is short lived. As trich is a waxing and waning condition, it is hard to tell if the improvement is a "placebo" effect (a result of the child "expecting" to get better with the medication), whether it is a function of the natural ups and downs of trich, or whether the medication is truly responsible.

Frequently, kids who are depressed or anxious and pull when they are having these feelings may benefit from taking anti-depressant medications. Sometimes the trich is helped when other symptoms improve. If no other symptoms are present (like depression or anxiety), it is uncertain whether anti-depressant medications will be helpful in reducing urges to pull hair.

Currently (at the time of the printing of this book) there have been no medication studies concerning children with tri-chotillomania. The studies with adults have had minimal results, so there are no drug use guidelines for trichotillomania. All medication use for children is what is considered "off label" treatment (which means that the medication is being prescribed for a different use than it has been approved for by the FDA). Conversations with your child's psychiatrist will help you to make an informed decision.

Now, on to the behavioral treatment! When behavioral

treatment is conducted with a motivated child and a willing family, it IS successful. We see children and adolescents reduce and stop pulling their hair all the time. Much like a diet and exercise program, however, it takes time, effort, and energy.

We have already talked a lot about how best to "parent" a child with trich. In behavioral treatment, a good therapist will work with you, as parents, to avoid IMPATIENCE, BLAMING, POLICING, and TOO MUCH FOCUS on hair. The key to parenting a child with trich is simple: accept and love your child as he/she is. A therapist working with your child will also add the following essential components:

1. Assessing all sensory, cognitive, affective, motor, and situational components of a child's hair pulling, after which a "functional analysis" or "behavioral analysis" is designed.

2. Tailoring the intervention by choosing specific coping strategies based upon the information from the functional analysis.

3. Evaluating what interventions work with a particular child.

4. Developing a plan for long-term maintenance of treatment gains and relapse prevention.

The first several sessions of treatment are spent not only educating parents and helping them to be less reactive, but also helping the child to be more aware of his/her behavior. Remember back in Chapter 1 we talked about the five components that contributed to a child's pulling behavior? This next section will flesh out what those components are and why we pay such close attention to them.

Sensory aspects of pulling

Although trich is different for each individual, people report some common experiences. The first area to be evaluated in therapy is the sensory component of pulling. All of the senses can be involved in the pulling process (touch, sight, taste, smell, and hearing).

Let's take a look at touch. Many people report pulling because of sensations that are experienced in the fingers before, during, or as a result of pulling. For example, it is common for children to enjoy the way that pulling the hair through their fingers feels. Sometimes they isolate hairs with certain textures (coarse, thick, wiry, curly, thin, bumpy) that give the tips of the fingers a particular sensation. It is common for people to stroke their hair prior to pulling or to run the hair through their fingers after it is pulled. All of these behaviors address the sense of touch. Over the years we have noticed that people who pull have amazing tactile sensitivity. They are able to feel subtle differences between hairs and to differentiate between hairs that are "good" to pull versus those that "should be left alone."

The second sensation that we look at is visual. Sometimes children are searching visually for hair with certain qualities, such as color (darker or lighter), texture (coarser, thicker, or bumpier), or some other aspect of the hair that is unusual (i.e., hairs that stick out, are curly or straightened, have split ends, or just somehow look different). With regard to eyelashes and eyebrows, visual triggers are common. Sometimes mirrors are used to identify hairs that are irregular, making bathrooms high risk places.

For many people with trich, the visual aspects of pulling occur after the hair is pulled. The hair or the bulb at the tip of the hair is frequently examined and analyzed. Many people report pulling hairs that they believe will have a large bulb. It is common for children to play with the hair or the bulb. Many people pull off the bulb or rub the bulb along their face or mouth (a touch sensation).

The sensations of taste, smell, and hearing are less common, but still evaluated in children with trich. About 13% of people report biting or eating the bulb and/or the whole hair (a taste sensation). Eating hair in large quantities can be dangerous to the digestive tract; consequently, a good therapist will always ask about hair ingestion. Sometimes hair has an odor that is interesting to a child and will lead to smelling the hair either before or after the hair is pulled. For some youngsters it is the sound of the hair being pulled out or the bulb being "popped" in the mouth that is motivating. All of these sensory experiences are important to evaluate. Once evaluated, the therapist will select specific coping strategies that will either help the child to satisfy their sensory needs in a manner other than pulling or to decrease the availability of the sensory stimulus, thus decreasing the sensory trigger that leads to pulling.

Thoughts are important too

Sometimes children develop beliefs or automatic thoughts that can lead to pulling. Thoughts may be permission giving, such as "I will just pull this one" or "I deserve this," or they can be mistaken beliefs about hair pulling, such as "I can't focus without pulling" or "I have to get all of the split ends out or I will look bad." Evaluating these thoughts and beliefs can lead to simple and effective interventions.

Thoughts can also be perfectionistic, such as "All of my eyelashes must be pointing the same way" or "This eyebrow must match the other exactly."   Understanding maladaptive thoughts or faulty beliefs can lead to specific, helpful strategies for behavior change, and constitute the "cognitive" in the cognitive behavioral model of therapy.

How feelings play a part

As discussed in Chapter 1, the DSM-IV diagnosis of trichotillomania requires that a person experience tension prior to pulling and gratification or relief during hair pulling behavior. However, studies have demonstrated that many other feelings precede pulling and a host of other emotions are experienced during and after an episode. Dr. Gretchen Deifenbach and her colleagues found that some people with trich pull when they are experiencing boredom, sadness, worry, or frustration. Children often pull when they feel overwhelmed, confused (i.e., in class), bored, angry, tired, or excited. In addition, pulling can result in feelings of relaxation, happiness, calmness, or even increased energy or concentration. Unfortunately, hair pulling can result in feelings of frustration, anger, guilt, and shame, which can leave a child at risk for another episode. Helping a child understand and eventually better manage emotional states can be essential in helping them to combat trich.

Busy hands

Many children with trich have a higher than normal need to fiddle or play with things in their hands. These kids always have something in hand—and sometimes it is hair. If this is the case, strategies are employed to keep the hands busy, to avoid putting them in the hair. Strategies are particularly useful if they are tailored to meet any "touch" preferences that may be present. For example, playdough, pipe cleaners, koosh balls, and bubble wrap are all useful "hand toys" that not only keep a child's hands busy, but also provide interesting textures and sensations on the fingers and hands. As we will see, one key to successful management of hair pulling is to encourage and reward alternative behaviors, rather than focusing on the hair or the pulling itself.

Environmental triggers and acquired habits

Although current theories explain that hair pulling is more complex than simply a "habit," there is still a "habitual" component to the behavior for many children. Hair pulling tends to occur in certain predictable situations for children. Situations can be a time of day, a place, or an activity. Most children can name two or three central places or activities where they tend to pull. Common hair pulling places may include the bedroom, bathroom, car, classroom, or den.

Activities that are commonly associated with pulling include trying to fall asleep, working on the computer, getting ready for bed, sitting on the toilet, sitting in the backseat of the car on a long trip, listening to a boring or confusing lecture in school, reading, studying, talking on the phone, or watching TV. Sometimes children only pull when they are alone, which can be a trigger in and of itself. Some pull in front of other people, but are discreet about how they do it. Most often, hair pulling takes place during sedentary activities. Knowing where and when hair pulling takes place is wonderful information so that coping strategies can be made available in these high risk situations.

It just feels good!

Whereas most of us would say that pulling out one's hair is painful, people with trich report physical sensations that are pleasant, interesting, or relieve discomfort. In reality, why would anyone pull if it hurt? The truth is, to those with trich, it feels very good. Some children report physical pleasure with pulling, such as tingling or soothing sensations on the skin. Other young people describe itching, burning, or discomfort on the skin prior to pulling that is somehow relieved by the removal of hair. The relief of the bad sensation is, therefore, very reinforcing. In either case, hair pulling provides very real relief or satisfaction to the puller.

Completing the assessment

To complicate matters, most children report many combinations of all of these sensory, cognitive, motor, emotional, and situational experiences. These combinations of experiences require a complex and individualized approach to treatment. For example, a child may sometimes pull when getting ready for bed (in the bathroom, tired, gazing in the mirror, and visually searching for curly hairs). That same child might also pull when in class (bored, hand near the head, feeling for coarse hairs). These two high risk situations require completely different interventions. Once the assessment is complete, appropriate strategies, such as behavioral substitutes, sensory distractions, coping techniques, relaxation strategies, and cognitive restructuring may be selected to help the child in his/her high risk situations.

Evaluation and positive reinforcement

After suggesting a variety of interventions to be tried over the course of several weeks, the therapist, child, and (sometimes) the parent will evaluate what is working and what is not working for the child. Adjustments and modifications will be made, as needed over time. Key strategies are identified along the way, and the child is positively reinforced for the use of strategies.

It is very important to remember that the focus should be on the *use of strategies, not hair growth.* If a child is using strategies, the hair pulling behavior will decrease and the hair will grow. If hair growth is used as the measure of success, the child is potentially being set up for failure. For example, a child can do really well for weeks, then have a setback and pull out most of the new growth. One could look at the scalp and say, "You are doing poorly and not making progress," when the reality is that the child has been doing really well, despite one difficult episode. In therapy we often say, "don't let a bad six minutes or six hours erase a good six weeks!"

So how does this work? A good therapist will set up a plan of action including all of the coping strategies that have been identified as potentially useful and those that are actually being used. The child will then pick some reward that he/she is willing to work to receive. It can be helpful to use stickers or tick marks on a calendar each day for the use of strategies, i.e., wearing Band Aids or using squeezy toys. When the child has accumulated a certain number of stickers or tick marks, the reward is given. Keeping the goals short-term is best, as a child will lose interest if the reward is too far off in the future. Start with daily or weekly rewards that over time can be stretched to longer periods of time. Each reward should be age appropriate. Stickers may work well for younger children and extra TV or computer time may work better for older kids. No matter what the age of your child, children like to receive verbal and concrete positive reinforcement, and this oftentimes is more meaningful to them than hair growth.

Long-term maintenance and relapse prevention

Setbacks are inevitable and to be expected. It is normal for a child to have times of success, followed by times of increased pulling. When you expect that setbacks are inevitable, they will be less disappointing and, consequently, your child will feel less like a failure. As with a diet program, you might do really well for a time, then for no real reason fall off the wagon and eat unhealthy foods. After a while, your motivation increases and you get back on track. Trich works in much the same way. Sometimes there is no specific reason why a child increases pulling—it just seems to happen.

That being said, there are predictable times that hair pulling seems to increase and decrease for kids. During summer and other school breaks, hair pulling tends to improve. The lack of school pressure and homework may be partly responsible for this improvement. Predictable times of setback include back to school in the fall, mid-terms, and final exam times. Also, it is important to be mindful of transitions, i.e., changing schools, moving to a new town, family changes, etc. Prepare your child for times that may be difficult.

Not all children are this predictable, though. Some youngsters do better with the structure of school and tend to relapse during winter and summer break when there is more free time and less structure in the day. Know your child and his/her pattern of behavior so that you can help him/her to be prepared for the times that may be difficult.

Slips versus relapse

The relapse prevention literature makes clear distinctions between a "slip" and a "relapse." A slip is a temporary return to a previous behavior, i.e., pulling a few hairs after having a period of no pulling. A relapse, on the other hand, is a return to the previous level of functioning, i.e., going back to regular intervals of pulling without the use of coping strategies. Parents should keep in mind that slips are normal and to be expected. The goal of treatment is to try to prevent a slip from turning into a relapse. When a slip occurs, handle it with care and finesse to prevent the dreaded relapse from following.

How do you do this? When a slip happens, it is helpful to encourage your child to take an investigative approach. Your child may need to ask key questions in a problem-solving manner. Questions might include:

- When did it happen?
- What was different about this situation?
- What strategies did I use?
- What strategies could I have used?
- What might I do differently next time?
- Has something changed?

⊙ Do I need to alter my coping strategies in certain situations?

⊙ What did I learn from this experience?

The last question is perhaps the most important. Your child can use a slip as a learning experience, one that will lead to better coping in the future. It may be helpful to refocus your child on goals and strategies, empathize with your child, and provide support. Remember, we have all experienced setbacks in behavior change and this is no different. Pay attention to how you feel; your child will sense your feelings and might take responsibility for them. Stay positive and solution-focused and your child will get back on track much faster. Managing trich is a process, a journey that has ups and downs. Ride the ups and downs like a car on the road. Treat each setback as a learning opportunity and your child will learn to do the same, without judgment or shame.

In sum, the treatment for trich is quite individualized. A good therapist will be able to tailor treatment appropriately for the age and unique qualities of your child. We hope that the overview of treatment has provided you with enough information to make an informed decision when looking for help. Regardless of whether or not you seek treatment for your child at this time, exploring and understanding your own feelings will be enormously helpful. In this next chapter we will look at some important points to consider when deciding how to move forward.

8
How to Help, Not Hurt

Mistakes are inevitable

More often than not parents start the process of dealing with their child's trichotillomania by making mistakes. Rarely do parents bring their child to treatment and not admit to making some common errors in their approach. This section will review some general and specific suggestions for you to successfully assist your child with hair pulling and, more importantly, to help him/her grow and develop as a healthy, emotionally strong child.

Loving acceptance

Probably the most important thing you can do to help your child is to love and accept him/her for who your child is, regardless of the hair pulling. Hair pulling is not life threatening (unless your child eats large quantities of hair) and help is out there. You must keep some perspective about the behavior, or it can become the center of a disastrous situation for the entire family. As seen with Stu and Karen, once they focused on accepting and loving Sarah with trichotillomania, Sarah, in turn, was able to accept and love herself.

Accepting your child with trichotillomania is probably the single most important thing that you can do. This will involve more work for you than for your child. Recognize your negative behaviors (comments, looks, sighs, emotional withdrawal) and commit to changing them. Instead of saying "Stop it!" pledge to say "I love you" or "Can I help you?" Learn to take a time out when you feel frustrated or angry, see a therapist, or talk to a friend when you are feeling down or at wits end. Make sure that you are commenting on many aspects of your child's life other than hair. Make sure you recognize things that your child excels at, such as sports, academics, and hobbies. In sum, it is your job to remain positive during this time of frustration and helplessness, which is not an easy task.

Educate yourself (and possibly your child too)

Another thing that you might do to help is to educate yourself and, if your child is receptive, to educate him/her as well. The fact that you are reading this book shows that you are doing some excellent self-study. If your child is open to talking about trich, you may want to explore some information with him/her. For example, facts you may want to share with your child are as follows:

1　Many people have trich.

2　Trich is common.

3　Many kids pull out their hair.

4　There is help available.

One amazing thing you can do for your child is to take him/her to a Trichotillomania Learning Center (TLC) Conference or Retreat where the whole family can learn about trich and be with others (both parents and children) who have similar experiences. This kind of intensive experience fosters self-acceptance and encourages readiness for change in children and parents. It also allows you and your child to meet some wonderful people who have something in common with you.

Your child may not yet be open to talking about trich. That's fine, too. You may still want to educate yourself or to simply talk to your child about what you have learned so far. Leaving some reading material around the house may also be useful. Sometimes it feels too "weird" to talk to a parent about trich. In this day of computers and Internet resources, you can provide your child with good information from respected web-sites, such as TLC, www.trich.org. Providing information will allow your child to educate him/herself in a manner that is not intimidating.

Who exactly is ready, you or your child?

It is often important to assess your child's willingness to enter therapy or even to work on changing his/her behavior. Not all children, especially adolescents, are ready to begin this process of behavior change by entering therapy or talking about hair pulling. More importantly, some parents can reach a point of readiness far earlier than their children. Be careful not to push your adolescent to change when he/she is not at the point of readiness. All too often, pushing a child too soon can result in the child pushing back. Remember, your child may not see hair pulling as a problem. Encouraging your child to come to one session in order to hear some information regarding trich from a professional can sometimes be a catalyst for change, and is sometimes all he/she is willing to do.

If your child is ready to enter therapy, find a therapist who is familiar with trich or at the very least is willing to learn about the treatment process. Many therapists are willing to read and obtain extra training. Contact TLC at www.trich.org

to find out if there is a trained therapist in your area. If not, start calling around and see if you can find someone who is willing to learn. Also, be willing to learn about yourself through the therapy process. You can, and should, learn about yourself, your reactions to your child's hair pulling, and specific ways to be helpful. Improving your reactions, your perspective, and your attitude toward your child will be one of the most important keys to your child's recovery from trich.

Unfortunately, there are many parts of the country where there are truly no therapists familiar with trichotillomania and its treatment. If you live in one of these areas there are a few resources still available to you. Some children and families can benefit from using the book, "The Hair Pulling 'Habit' and You: How to Solve the Trichotillomania Puzzle." This self-help book is written for children, adolescents, and adults and is presented in a very easy to follow manner. It is a treatment guide that uses the model for treatment discussed in this book. Sometimes therapists who may not be familiar with trich, but who are interested in learning, will utilize the book in the course of therapy.

If using a book does not work for you or your child, a very helpful website, www.stoppulling.com, can provide information, guidance, suggestions, and feedback on progress. For children who are computer users, this website helps the child track the pulling behaviors, and then guides the child to employ appropriate coping strategies. In addition, it also provides visual feedback, graphs reflecting progress, and many useful suggestions. So even though a knowledgeable therapist may not be available, some interesting and helpful options do exist.

This is a process, be patient and understanding

Another very important thing to know about having a child with trich is that the process of managing hair pulling is just that—a process. Many people with trich who learn to cope with urges think "OK, I'm done, no need to worry about that anymore." Well, the truth is that trich is a high relapse behavior. Without consistent follow-up and attention, many children relapse. As stated in Chapter 7, relapse often occurs at times of stress or times of change. Typical times include changing schools, going to college, ending or beginning of the semester, moving to another city or state, or significant family changes. Change or stress does not guarantee that relapse will occur, but it is important to be prepared, and to prepare your child.

We often explain to clients that management of hair

pulling is much like management of weight. If I go on a diet and exercise program and lose 40 pounds in six months, I do not then go back to eating whatever I want and become sedentary again. If I do, what will happen? I will gain all of my weight back! The same idea applies to trich. A person cannot get pulling under control and then step back and forget all about it—he/she must continue with the program. Much like the weight management scenario, it gets easier and easier to "maintain," but one must still stay aware and remain focused.

After a person has gotten pulling under control, it is still important to use strategies, identify high risk situations, anticipate difficult times, and set goals. Managing trichotillomania is a process that must be incorporated into daily life, as opposed to a goal that will be reached, completed—and forgotten.

When and how do I get involved?

One of the most common questions parents ask is "How can I help my child?" The answer has everything to do with your child and his/her individual wishes. In therapy we always ask children what they think would be helpful. Sometimes children do not want their parents to say anything about their hair—not to check on progress, not to nag, and not to recommend strategies for them to use. Often, children will try this "going it alone" and then decide that they might, in fact, need some kind of help. It's important to be flexible and allow your child to change his/her mind about how involved you might be from week to week until you discover a process that works for you and your child.

Sometimes, children will ask their parents to help them become aware of when they are pulling or at risk to pull. We like to come up with "secret phrases" or "secret signals" that indicate the need to be alert to hair pulling. Let your child be the author of these phrases or signals if they are interested. Be careful to use these phrases and signals in discreet ways, not to shame or humiliate your child.

Often children like to sit down at the end of the day and put a sticker on the calendar with their parent. The sticker might represent how they did that day. If they used their coping strategies in high risk situations, they might get a sticker that says "awesome!" If the day was hard, they might get a "keep on trying!" sticker. Allow your child to craft the "sticker process" and to develop the meaning for the different stickers. This will encourage the use of strategies and, eventually will lead to more effective management of hair pulling.

After reading and learning about interventions for trich, allow your child to give input on what feels good to him/her.

With the assistance of a therapist, your child may request that you take a less active roll in the treatment. If this is the case, it is important to respect your child's wishes.

Finally, many times parents may feel the need to change their child. Having a child with trichotillomania is uniquely challenging. Parents may feel as if they are doing a poor job parenting due to their child's hair pulling. As a result, some parents may try to force change upon their child. This can be extremely hard on the child, the parents, and the entire family. Although at times difficult, it is most helpful to allow your child to be who he/she is. Rejoice in your child's strengths and celebrate his/her abilities. Accept this uniqueness instead of fighting against it. If you can do this, you will be able to enjoy your child and the process of parenting on a much deeper level.

Every parent faces unique challenges in parenting. These challenges have to do with the number of children you may have, their ages, your ages, your model for parenting, the temperament of your child, and many other issues too numerous to mention. Add to this list hair pulling, and you find yourself in a poorly understood, isolated, unique group. In this final chapter we will revisit the cases discussed earlier in this book and will bring you up to date on their individual journeys.

9
The End of the Story

The long haul

So, what happens to children who learn to manage their trich? Do they stay pull-free forever? Do they relapse? These are great questions that have yet to be answered in the research. There are no long-term studies of children who received treatment for trich early in life and were evaluated later in adulthood. Thus, we have no scientific research to predict what the long-term affect of early treatment might be. What we do know is what is commonly reported in therapy. This chapter will revisit the case examples discussed earlier in the book to see what happens to these kids down the road.

Ashley

For Ashley, it took her parents' understanding of her behavior to help them cope and eventually assist her calmly and compassionately with behavior change. Over the years, Ashley engaged in other body focused repetitive behaviors. She started biting her fingernails at age six and this continued until age eight. Her parents took much the same approach with this behavior as they did with her trich. They identified common situations where the biting occurred and provided other, alternative coping skills for her, such as hand-held games and Band Aids. This worked very well.

Over the years, it became obvious that Ashley was a very fidgety kid who grew into a fidgety adult. She picked at napkins, bent paperclips, and ripped labels off of soda bottles. She did lots of things with her hands while sitting still. Although she bit her fingernails and fidgeted with almost anything, she never pulled her hair again.

Sarah

Sarah did well in treatment throughout second and third grades. She remained pull-free through middle school and high school, but had a setback her freshman year in college. Sarah had very few memories of her earlier bout with trich. She remembered her therapist and liking therapy, but not much about what they discussed.

Sarah attended her first TLC Retreat as an adult the fall of her sophomore year in college. She met other young adults with trich and many professionals who encouraged her to work hard and who helped her to laugh again. *"It was amazing to meet other people with trichotillomania! I felt so validated and happy. I now have many friends around the country who have trich. We text daily to see how we are all doing. Sometimes we text each other if we are having a hard time and help each other out of an episode. I am so lucky to have so many friends who understand me and are willing to take the time to help me when I need it."*

Although she has no bald spots anymore, Sarah still pulls. She is so good at monitoring her pulling, though, that she is able to stop herself if she goes beyond ten hairs in a day. Instead of beating herself up after an episode, she takes a deep breath and says "It's OK, let's figure out what is wrong and make it better." Her acceptance that urges are going to happen and that she does not have to yield to them has helped her experience success. *"If you ask me, I am in remission. I pull once or twice a month, but it is never more than a few. Sometimes I even giggle at myself for going with the urge instead of doing something else—it is like a game to me now."*

Sarah is a great example of true management of trichotillomania over time. She has accepted that sometimes she will experience urges to pull. Instead of wishing that she would not have urges or trying to make them go away, she understands that they are a part of who she is, which helps her deal with them as they occur.

◉

Hannah

Remember Hannah? She started to pull her hair in early adolescence. Hannah began by pulling her pubic hair and eventually moved to pulling scalp hair. Her parents, Peggy and Bob, found help through the TLC and were able to focus less on hair and more on other aspects of Hannah's life. Hannah did end up in behavior therapy for trichotillomania and self-esteem issues. She learned different ways to think about herself and about life. She became more optimistic about her future and about her ability to cope with pulling urges and episodes.

Hannah has graduated from college and is working in a large urban area. She has been pull-free since her junior year in high school. *"I remember how mad I was at my parents for not understanding. I hated them because I thought they loved me less for pulling. They were constantly on me, riding me about my hair. Finally, I just wanted to scream 'Stay out of my hair!' But they learned and they got better. Today, I don't pull, but I still play with my hair constantly. I guess I know that it is still a possibility, but I just don't go there. My life is so awesome right now I just say to myself, 'What are you thinking?*

You have worked so hard to get here…don't go back!'"

Hannah attends the TLC retreat every year and keeps up with friends in the trich world. She is an inspiration for many young people who are still struggling and has expressed interest in becoming a therapist someday. *"I would love to help people with trich and other body focused repetitive behaviors, like I got help. I want to give back because so many people have given to me over the years. I am no different from other people who pull, I just haven't done it in a long time."*

Hayden

Hayden went to a small liberal arts college on a basketball scholarship. Shortly into his freshman year, his hair pulling resumed. He felt a lot of pressure from academics, athletics, and from juggling the two. Hayden went to the Student Counseling Center and found a therapist who was a good fit for him. Although no one at the Counseling Center knew how to treat trich, this therapist had heard of it and was willing to learn.

Hayden became aware that just as he had started pulling in high school to soothe himself around his sadness about his parents' divorce, he was soothing himself now. Again, Hayden had to learn strategies to cope with feelings of frustration, anxiety, and fear of failure. Once again, he was successful.

Hayden graduated with honors and went on to get a Master's degree in Business Administration. He is currently employed with a large financial firm and is pull-free. *"As much as I hated it, I am glad I went through having trich. I think I have more empathy for people who have habits that are hard to change. I see people trying to change their diets or to quit smoking and I think...I completely understand. They are just trying to feel better...just like I was. If I have a child with trichotillomania, I will be there for him, I will support him because I understand what it feels like. My parents didn't know, but I will."*

Moving forward

We hope this book has been a source of good information and greater understanding of your feelings, of your reactions, and of your child's hair pulling. Our goal has been to provide information about trich to help you gain perspective and to give you strength and courage to move forward. Although trich can be frustrating, angering, and sometimes hopelessly exhausting, it can also be a turning point for you and your family.

Instead of fighting the presence of trich in your life, accept that it just IS in your life. Once you can do that, you can begin to make positive changes for you, your child, and your family. Christina Pearson, the Executive Director and founder of the Trichotillomania Learning Center, once said the following, which applies to parents as much as it does to children struggling with trich: "You are not responsible for the fact that you [or your child] have trichotillomania, but you are responsible for how you approach it. You can either choose to be a victim, or learn to walk with grace." Let this moment be the beginning of your graceful journey.

Bibliography

American Psychiatric Association. (1994). *Diagnostic and Statistical Manual of Mental Disorders (4th ed.)*. Washington, DC.

Azrin, N. H., & Nunn, R. G. (1973). *Habit-reversal: A method of eliminating nervous habits and tics. Behaviour Research and Therapy, 11,* 619-628.

Christenson, G. A., Pyle, R. L., & Mitchell, J. E. (1991). *Estimated lifetime prevalence of trichotillomania in college students. Journal of Clinical Psychiatry, 52,* 415-417.

Diefenbach, G.J., Mouton-Odum, S., & Stanley, M.A. (2002). *Affective correlates of trichotillomania. Behaviour Research and Therapy, 40,* 1305-1315.

Franklin, M. E., Flessner, C. A., Woods, D. W., Keuthen, N. J.., Piacentini, J. C., Moore, P. S., Stein, D. J., Cohen, S., & The Trichotillomania Learning Center Scientific Advisory Board (in press). *The Child and Adolescent Trichotillomania Impact Project (CA-TIP): Exploring descriptive psychopathology, functional impairment, comorbidity, and treatment utilization. Journal of Developmental and Behavioral Pediatrics.*

Mansueto, C. S., Golomb, R. G., Thomas, A. M., & Stemberger, R. M. T. (1999). *A comprehensive model for behavioral treatment of trichotillomania. Cognitive and Behavioral Practice, 6,* 23-43.

Rothbaum, B. O., Shaw, L., Morris, R., & Ninan, P. T. (1993). *Prevalence of trichotillomania in a college freshman population. Journal of Clinical Psychiatry, 54,* 72-73.

Stanley, M. A., Borden, J. W., Bell, G. E., & Wagner, A. L. (1994). *Nonclinical hair-pulling: Phenomenology and related psychopathology. Journal of Anxiety Disorders, 8,* 119-130.

Resources

Websites:

www.trich.org

www.stoppulling.com

Books:

The Hair Pulling "Habit" and You:

How to Solve the Trichotillomania Puzzle

by Ruth Golomb and Sherrie Vavrichek

The Hair Pulling Problem

by Fred Penzel

Help for Hair Pullers

by Nancy Keuthen, Dan J. Stein,
and Gary Christenson

About the Authors

Suzanne Mouton-Odum

Suzanne Mouton-Odum, Ph.D. is a psychologist in private practice in Houston, Texas. She obtained her doctoral degree from The University of Houston in Counseling Psychology and completed her residency in Clinical Psychology at the University of Texas Medical School in Houston. She has treated people with trich and other body focused repetitive behaviors since 1993 and has been a member of the Trichotillomania Learning Center Scientific Advisory Board since 2001. Dr. Mouton-Odum regularly attends and presents at the TLC Annual Conference and Retreat. She is the co-owner and lead developer of the only interactive, on-line website for trichotillomania, www.stoppulling.com and for skin picking disorders, www.stoppicking.com. She is happily married and lives in Houston with her husband and two children.

Ruth Goldfinger Golomb

Ruth Goldfinger Golomb, LCPC, is a senior clinician, supervisor, and a director of the doctoral training program at the Behavior Therapy Center of Greater Washington, where she has worked since the mid-1980's. Ms. Golomb specializes in treatment of anxiety disorders in children and adults. She has conducted numerous workshops and seminars, and participated as an expert in panel discussions covering many topics, including Tourette Syndrome, Obsessive Compulsive Disorder, Trichotillomania, and managing anxiety disorders in the classroom. She also has attended the national TLC conferences and retreats since the mid-1990's. In addition to publishing articles for professional journals and newsletters, Ms Golomb is an author of "The Hair Pulling 'Habit' and You: How to Solve the Trichotillomania Puzzle," a book describing the comprehensive treatment of trichotillomania in children.

Ms. Golomb is member of the Science Advisory Board for The Trichotillomania Learning Center. She is also happily married and lives in the Washington, D.C. area with her husband and two children.